Congo
Dawn

· · · · · · · · · · · · · · · ·

John B. Franz

outskirtspress
DENVER, COLORADO

Contents

Acknowledgments

During the course of the Viet Nam War, some 170,000 young men received conscientious objector (CO) deferments and like me, performed alternate service rather than participating as soldiers in that controversial conflict. Over the intervening years, conversations with CO peers have alerted me to the fact that many of us share a common sentiment: the direction of our lives has been greatly impacted by our alternate service experiences.

My story thus illuminates a parallel process that quietly took place in our culture during the 1960s, often out of the public eye. Conscientious objectors were still stigmatized in those days. Our stories have subsequently received little acknowledgment and have drawn minimal attention in comparison to the dramatic and horrific tales of combat veterans or even the angst-laced stories of draft evaders. This memoir is a small step toward validating the contributions of those who served their country and their conscience as pacifists, and toward identifying how their lives were changed by their years of alternate service.

I've long felt that my experiences in the Congo as a young man needed to be captured and examined a bit more closely. The memories and insights from those days have periodically flittered across my consciousness much like the wild birds in our back yard – branch to feeder to ground and then away. While I have found it entertaining and sometimes amusing to witness the appearance of these winged memories from time to time, I have carried within a clear sense that my so-called "Congo stories" deserve more than a casual glance. I have long believed, without careful examination, that many of the things I value most in my life were created or shaped during my initial sojourn in Africa. This memoir has provided the opportunity to take that second look, to recognize my experiences as more than a series of separate events – as a character-shaping force.

I would like to recognize Jim Becker, my partner and roommate in the Congo and lifelong friend, as the source of my motivation to write this memoir. His instructional writing project "The Great Adventure" was shared with me as a challenge to move our story past merely describing the departure. Jim has continued to encourage and clarify my descriptions and memories as I have responded to his challenge.

Fellow TASOK teacher and University of Minnesota

archivist, David Klaassen, has been a welcome companion in this project, offering anecdotes, information and observations from one who was there. Similarly, former travel mates and teaching colleagues, Garry and Lois Schmidt have shared their perspectives, memories and photos from our Congo years together.

Retired English teachers, Wilfred Martens and Ron Horton, have read and offered valuable suggestions to improve my story-telling capacity. I also acknowledge the helpful encouragement and feedback of friends Wes Thiessen and Larry Martens who have read, responded and made me feel appreciated rather than embarrassed for exposing my youthful foibles.

Finally, and especially, I'd like to acknowledge the encouragement and support of my wife and best friend of more than four decades, Betty Jean. She is fearless in her feedback, gifted in her ability to catch errant details, and wonderfully authentic and generous in her love and commitment to me. I keep telling her I had to travel halfway across the world to find her, but it was worth every bit of the effort!

Introduction

———⫸⫷———

"It is while you are patiently toiling at the little tasks of life that the meaning and shape of the great whole of life dawn on you."
– Phillip Brooks

The challenge in getting one's act together for the first time as an adult is how to do it. First times are like that. There is a sense of urgency, to be sure, and a strong pull in the direction of independence, but few clues about how to actually make it happen. What kind of a person do I want to be? What should I do with my life? To whom and what should I commit myself? What am I good at? How can I make a difference, be successful? What should I do next?

It seems that young adulthood is often accompanied by more questions than answers. In my case, it was also accompanied by a healthy dose of youthful hubris and motivated by a thirst for adventure. These qualities animated the period for me. Truthfully, the mix also included an ample supply of courage, energy and naiveté, comingled. All of these elements made their appearance in my particular journey toward manhood.

This memoir describes a time of transition in my young adult life as I began to formulate my first adult life structure. The concept of a life structure originated with Yale psychologist, Daniel Levinson. He proposed a comprehensive theory of adult development, popularized in his seminal book, *Seasons of a Man's Life.* Central to Levinson's theory, life structure refers to the underlying pattern that defines a person's life at a given point in time. Shaped mainly by one's social and physical environment – primarily family and work – life structure is also influenced by other factors such as religion, race, education and economic status.

Levinson labeled this time of life – one's early 20s – *"Entering the adult world."* It is an era of making initial choices in the areas of friendships, values, lifestyle, occupation and love. Each developmental stage of life may be characterized by two phases: a stable period, when key decisions are made; and a transitional period, when the quality of one's life commitments changes. My experiences with transitioning into adulthood are described here.

What made the dawning of my enlightenment unique was its context: The Democratic Republic of the Congo, in West Africa, during the Viet Nam War in the mid-1960s.

1
Decisions, Decisions

"Choices are the hinges of destiny."
– Pythagoras

I t was spring, 1966, and my 21-year-old head was full of turmoil. Just weeks away from college graduation, final exams were looming like dark clouds on the horizon. They weren't the only threats in sight, however. I had some big decisions facing me.

On the surface, my mid-60s college world looked pretty good. A letterman's jacket (basketball), pre-med major and prom princess girl friend illustrated that point. The Momma's and Papa's, Righteous Brothers and the Supremes soothed my troubled mind with their mellow musical reflections, but dissonant tones had begun to invade my fragile reality. Barry Sadler's #1 hit of 1966, *The Ballad of the Green Berets*, was a blunt reminder that Viet Nam was calling young men like me.

My apparently successful journey to graduation was colored by the unexpected consequence of *"having to decide."* The specter of the military draft imposed a limited set of options as the arrival of commencement cancelled my educational deferment. Whatever the compelled decision turned out to be, my choice was likely to be *life changing.*

With lofty ambitions, four years earlier I had entered the University of Oregon in my hometown of Eugene. As a Student Body President and an All-State track and basketball player in high school the trappings of success were there. Awarded the university's "Order of the O" scholarship as the year's most promising freshman grant-in-aid athlete, high hopes of future success loomed before me. I boldly declared a pre-med major and visualized myself as the next *"Dr. Kildare"* or *"Marcus Welby, MD,"* to confess the true TV sources of my career selection. A wealth of social opportunities accompanied my status as a college athlete in the years that followed.

These facts painted a rosy picture as I entered college. By my senior year on campus, however, a different image emerged. I was more often a bench warmer than a starter on the U of O basketball team. Mononucleosis wiped out my freshman season, and I was neither tall enough for a post man nor quick enough for a guard to be very effective in Division I competition. The academic courses for which I had the least affection or affinity were all in the sciences, my chosen major. I loved the social sciences but struggled at mastering organic chemistry formulas and memorizing comparative anatomy charts. Socially? My girlfriend's philosophy of life clashed with my core values – not a good match.

It seemed, then, that under close inspection, college had not fulfilled my aspirations on *any* of the main axes: academics, athletics, or social relationships. Unfortunately, there was no option for a "do-over."

Some say that the past is the best predictor of the future. If my college years fit the first half of that adage, it seems I was heading for *serious trouble*.

. . . .

My response to the military draft during the Viet Nam War era was surely informed and shaped by family. Dad had served as the West Coast director of Civilian Public Service (CPS) providing conscientious objectors (COs) an alternative to military service during the Second World War. My grandfather was a Mennonite pastor who nearly lost his life to a mob of drunken patriots during WWI due to his German accent and pacifist beliefs. CO service was my legacy.

Nevertheless, the decision to become a conscientious objector was, in the end, a personal choice. Mine was an active church-going family throughout my formative years and at a young age I made a declaration of faith in Jesus Christ. I was not particularly rebellious or defiant but as I grew up, my actions were not always consistent with my faith proclamations. Though a common pattern among teenage males, my inconsistent behavior suggested that I did not possess a mature spirituality. In spite of my immaturity, however, I genuinely identified as a believer and viewed the Bible as my prime source of how to live.

When it came time to fill out the required Selective Service questionnaire at age 18 my father took time to thoughtfully review with me the key questions and Biblical responses from a pacifist perspective. That meaningful exercise helped to define my Christian identity, at least at that stage of life. I became an enthusiastic pacifist.

As personal and deliberate as was my choice of Biblical non-resistance, in retrospect, there were other non-religious influences at play, as well. Lifestyle decisions are products not only of our family and personal beliefs but also of our cultural context. This issue was no exception. Many of my generation – particularly those attending college – were strongly opposed to the Viet Nam War, though not from Biblical beliefs. This fact no doubt contributed to my choice of Selective Service options other than military service.

Some weeks after my 18th birthday, official conscientious objector status was conferred and the associated "1-0" classification was issued to me by my local draft board. In 1966, draftees were inducted by birthdate, rather than by a lottery. Three years later all draftees were assigned a draft lottery number, thereby enabling one to determine the likelihood of being inducted. Those with lower numbers had a high likelihood of being drafted in a given year, while birthdates with higher lottery numbers might see the quota filled and thereby avoid military service. No such mechanism was in place when I faced the draft. My cohort had to take its chances in planning a future.

I attended college on an educational deferment that was about to expire. Since I was over the optimal draft age of 19 years, I reasoned that I was more likely than not to be called up. Once I graduated from college, if drafted, my 1-O classification meant that I was facing two years of alternative service.

But what kind of service should I do? Where? As I approached commencement, the only answer that seemed clear to me was *"it should be somewhere far from here!"*

My home church was affiliated with the Mennonite Brethren (MB) denomination. As a historic peace church, both the MBs and related Mennonite organizations offered a number of options for fulfilling alternate service obligations to the government. I checked out a range of possibilities. I even considered joining the Peace Corps. I hoped to somehow incorporate my college degree in any service choice I would eventually make. After reviewing and discussing different possibilities with my parents and pastor, I finally made a decision.

I settled on the *Christian Service Program* sponsored

by the MBs. They were recruiting for a high school science and PE teaching position available in an American dependents' school in Kinshasa, Democratic Republic of the Congo, Africa. The assignment would make use of my college degree and athletic experience. Its location sounded like an exotic setting about as far from Oregon as I could imagine. About as far, culturally and geographically, as one can get. *A real adventure!*

My young, idealistic, curious, 21-year-old self sought distance from all the familiar sameness of home. I felt anxious to try out life and be my own person, distanced from the flawed expectations and disillusionment of adolescence. College hadn't turned out as I expected. Maybe a change for the better was coming up. Maybe it was just time to do something really different – break with the old and take on the new. Emancipate. Teaching in Africa seemed like a great way to begin adult life.

Acceptance into the Christian Service Program required an official application, reference letters, a physical exam and a good deal of anxious waiting. All of these factors I managed to fit into my final term of college. One by one each element was completed, and the application was submitted. Finally, a letter of acceptance arrived at my home in Eugene. This appeared to be an open door, but who knew what was on the other side.

Uncertainty – that's what turns an experience into an adventure. Shouldn't any portal to the future start with adventure? What an intense and exciting time of life.

Two years of teaching in Africa seemed like a *really good idea* at the time – in theory, that is. The reality, however, did not line up quite so nicely. I had never taken a single teacher education course. Having lived exclusively in Eugene, Oregon, I had only traveled out of state for a few college basketball games. I had never really been around people who weren't a lot like me. I'd never lived on my own or resided anywhere I couldn't reach my parents – with a *local* phone call. In short, I was ill prepared for the challenges and adaptations before me.

That, of course, was an understatement. As former White House Chief of Staff and Defense Secretary, Donald Rumsfeld was to later remark in a classic quote, "There are things we do not know we don't know."

2

No Dodging the Draft

"Please Mr. Custer, I don't wanna go!"
– (War protest song popular in the 1960s)

I f my pacifist legacy and the national news weren't
enough to convince me of the folly of participation in
the Viet Nam War, then I received one more poignant
reminder in the form of an unwelcome and unexpectedly close encounter with the U. S Military Draft.

I passed my physical exam, applied for a passport,
obtained my yellow fever injections, and following
directions from the Christian Service (CS) program, re-
quested that my draft board "call up my number." By
requesting my file to be called up, I would thereby get
credit for my approved CO service.

Three weeks later I received the expected "Uncle Sam
wants you" form letter with a designated date for my
mandatory draft induction physical exam. In response, I
sent a registered letter to my local draft board – following

CS directions – indicating that I was respectfully *declining* to submit to the induction exam, since I had already been accepted into an alternative service program. My letter acknowledged that I understood the penalty for a "no show" was that I would be automatically inducted: the purpose/goal of my initial request to the board.

One week before my final exams, I received an angry, agitated phone call from the clerk of my local draft board. "Son, you are in big trouble!" she bluntly exclaimed. When I attempted to explain my actions, she angrily interrupted me with a threat: "If you fail to comply with this directive, I will send the sheriff to arrest you!" At that point, she abruptly hung up.

Flabbergasted and alarmed, I informed my parents of the call. After some discussion about steps I might take to respond to the clerk's demand, I reluctantly concluded that I was going to have to go through the whole induction process. They agreed. It seemed that my passage into the future would start down a one-way street I had not planned to traverse.

On the day of my last final exam, physics, my mother picked me up as I exited the science building on the U of O campus.

"How did you do on your final?" she asked.

"Lousy. I am way too distracted to calculate motion and force formulas."

Ever the optimist, Mom responded with a hopeful comment. "Don't be so gloomy, John. You might just be surprised how well you did."

"*This* is the exam I'm *really* dreading," I offered after a short pause, referring to the induction physical exam toward which we were headed.

"Well, it should at least make you thankful you don't have to actually *do* military service," she offered.

She was right.

Shortly, we arrived at the Eugene Greyhound Bus depot for the two-hour transport to Portland where the state's official draft induction center was located. I said my goodbyes and boarded the specially marked Greyhound bus.

I was one of the last to enter the bus. It was filled with loud, longhaired 19-year-olds. They seemed excited and their banter, raucous. I was relieved to have a seat to myself for the ride to Portland. I had a lot of things to ponder. Quietly. At the conclusion of the bus ride we draftees were given a cafeteria supper at the Portland YMCA.

We slept that night in bunks in the YMCA dorm. Perhaps it would be more accurate to say that we *spent the night* there, since judging from the ambient noise, few, including me, actually slept much. We arose the next morning and consumed a forgettable breakfast of dry toast, cold scrambled eggs and lukewarm coffee. As we finished eating, a quartet of tough-looking soldiers in army uniforms arrived to escort us to the induction center down the street.

The military induction facility consisted of a large assembly room that held perhaps 500 people, surrounded by smaller exam rooms where draftees were evaluated at a series of stations. My cohort of draftees crowded into the main assembly room. All the chairs were filled. All shapes, sizes and colors of young men packed the room, lining the aisles and walls.

I remember being surprised at the number of African American draftees present on that occasion, since there were few people of color in my hometown community. Where did they come from? Was the government somehow disproportionately drafting blacks, I wondered? Perhaps fewer people of color were successful at getting deferments, I concluded.

The nervous banter of the draftees buzzed around me. It was animated by a mixture of theories on how to avoid induction, co-mingled with tips on which branch of the service was best to join. I felt – all at the same time – *fearful and intimidated* as a "closet CO"; *resentful* at having to be there; and *sad*, imagining that soon many of my fellow draftees would be placed in harms' way. By June of 1966 the nightly news carried regular reports of the expanding specter of the Viet Nam War. Things appeared to be getting worse, not better.

My induction center companions came across as a motley and undisciplined assembly of characters. I found myself thinking the prideful thoughts of an ABC (All But Commencement) college grad. If "America's freedom" was to be defended by *this* representative collection of teenaged dropouts and misfits, perhaps we were *all* in more trouble than anyone realized!

After a few minutes, a stony-faced army sergeant called for silence. He got it. The noise level dropped instantly as all eyes turned in his direction. Apparently, others were as nervous and apprehensive as I felt. He barked directions to his anxious listeners before dismissing us from the assembly room to different examination stations. We filed out in groups of twenty or so. We were instructed to disrobe to our undershorts and place our clothes and shoes in the sack or small bag we had been told to bring with us. Even this small act seemed to strip away our identities and defenses. It was unsettling. There was more to come.

In the course of the day's exams, some of the potential draftees attempted to fake impairments to avoid induction. One young man with a crooked smile sat in the soundproof booth for testing hearing with the sensor button fully depressed throughout the entire test. Others walked up to within inches of the eye charts, dramatically squinting as if they could not make out the largest letters.

In the huge restroom, a draftee who claimed to have diabetes shared his fresh beaker of urine with others who eagerly solicited a few precious drops of the tainted elixir. Though I was in reality close to the induction height limit of 6'6", when it came time to measure me, I was officially recorded at only 6'3 ½". The army assistant doing the measuring simply slammed the metal slide down on my head so hard that it bent, yielding a shorter height.

An IQ exam consisted of simple math - adding/ subtracting - matching shapes and elementary school story problems. I wondered who *couldn't* pass such a slam-dunk test.

I pity the luckless army staffer assigned to do anal exams. One can only imagine the flatulent outcome of demanding reluctant draftees to "bend over and spread your cheeks" as a disgusted soldier slowly walked down the line, clipboard in hand, peering into the rear ends of his subjects.

Throughout the day there was a lot of yelling and cursing by the army staff that were performing the various exams, demanding compliance and confronting suspected "draft dodgers." In sum, it was a strange, surreal experience.

By the end of the afternoon, all 500+ of us were herded back into the main assembly room where we were informed of options available to inductees who had passed the induction physical. We were polled regarding our educational level. Having completed even a year of college qualified a draftee to volunteer for officer candidate training school. There were only four individuals in the entire room who indicated having taken *any* college courses, and I was the *only one* having completed four years. That surprised me.

Some draftees decided to volunteer for the Navy or Marines, rather than go into the Army. Apparently, it appealed to them to have at least some choice in how they fulfilled their service obligation. These individuals were ushered to busses that departed from the induction center and headed directly to basic training sites in California. No returning home to say "good-bye" for *these* last-chance "volunteers!"

As the meeting concluded and we stood to exit, a sergeant near the door barked at me, "You're in the US Army, now son, so *move it!*" "I'm never serving in *your* army," I thought, with a mixture of repulsion and relief. I rushed out of the room and boarded the bus for my return to Eugene.

Other than receiving my 1-W draft status change for entering alternate service, I never heard *anything* further from my draft board.

3
Severing Ties That Bind

"Nobody said it was easy; it's such a shame for us to part. Nobody said it was easy... no one ever said it would be this hard."
– Coldplay, "The Scientist"

The whole "tie severing" experience in those last couple of weeks before my departure for Africa was a mixed bag. Tie severing usually is, I've learned. In the crossroads of life I've come to thus far, one part of me is typically anxious to get on with "the next chapter," while another part wants to hold on to the familiar and the meaningful and not let go. Some crossroads encounters are mellow and joyful – fond farewells – while others are tearful, painful or complicated separations. Beginnings and endings *are* the most difficult parts of relationships.

I enjoyed the attention and the faintly disguised jealousy embedded in the questions and comments of my age peers when I finally started saying my good-byes.

"Are you *really* going to Africa?"

"Hasn't the Congo had a lot of turmoil – is it safe to go there?

"What will you do about the Draft? Oh."

"How long will you be gone?"

"Teaching sounds like a cool thing to do, but you haven't taken any education courses, have you?"

"Will you get to do any traveling when school isn't in session?"

"Aren't you worried about snakes, lions and malaria?"

Providing responses that were about as naive as the questions posed to me, it was clear my knowledge of Africa equaled that of teaching. In both cases it barely made the charts. My flippant replies suggested that I was undeterred in my youthful confidence, however.

"I probably won't see too much wild life in a city of five million people...*animal* wild life, that is."

"I've learned *a lot* about teaching over the years...as a student. Besides, *everyone* in my family is a teacher, so no sweat – it's in my blood!"

It seemed unreal that I would not see most of my friends in the same way ever again. I'm sure I failed to appreciate the finality of this transition point in my social world at the time. Some of them I would encounter once more, briefly, upon my return in two years; others, I would have no contact with for decades; a few ended their life journey early, so these visits were truly final events. Several of my classmates died in Viet Nam. Apparently, I'd be making my way into the future with new company.

One particular farewell sticks in my memory. Shortly after graduation, my roommate, Tim Pike, and I took a two-day backpacking trip into the Cascade Mountains above Eugene. We had become good friends during our senior year and we promised one another we'd share this final retreat before heading our separate ways.

Our post-graduation excursion also included our cat, Daphne, cynically named after one of our sexy instructors at the university. College male humor: "Who'd like to pet Daphne tonight?"

Don't take a house cat camping. Our daylight hours in the mountains were animated by hours of chasing that flaky feline through the forest or coaxing her down from trees she had scaled in panic. We laughed and swore and marveled at our stupidity in thinking it was a clever idea to backpack with a house cat. We also spent long, poignant hours into the night over our campfire philosophizing, speculating what the future might hold and wondering if we would still be friends when we got old.

A few weeks later Tim married his girl friend, Linda. Together, they entered the Peace Corps in Micronesia at about the same time I left for Africa. Tim died of leukemia in their second year there. I alone carried into adulthood those campfire dreams we confided in one another.

My parting visit with my girlfriend during the last week before I left would also be the last I'd have with her as our paths permanently diverged. It began to dawn on me that the time had arrived to begin a new chapter in my life.

Tim and fiancée Linda

It's true that one just never knows when a simple good-bye turns out to be a final event. My farewell conversations with my grandparents illustrated this point. In the final pre-departure weeks, I had separate in-depth visits with both of my grandmothers. One, widowed, had lived with us through my high school and college years, and the other resided with my grandfather in Salem, Oregon, an hour or so north of my Eugene home.

As I perceived it at the time, both grandmothers were unusually tender and emotional in their questions and affirmations of me. It wasn't until 18 months later, reading my mother's sad letter in my Kinshasa, Congo, apartment that I remembered that *both* grandmothers had made the *same point* to me – they each wondered out-loud if they'd ever see me again.

I found myself, in those visits, subtly distressed and almost annoyed by this grim proposition each grandmother presented to me. Rejecting their pessimistic reflections, I attempted to reassure them in my 22-year-old optimistic mindset: "We should not think sad thoughts, but rather look forward to seeing one another when I return. Then, I'll tell you in detail all about my adventures in Africa."

Little did I imagine that during the next two years of my Congo service, both of my grandmothers would pass away. It turned out that they were *both* right! Those final visits would indeed be my last with each of them.

These weren't the only goodbyes I needed to make. I also needed to terminate with Mom and Dad.

4
Preparing to Launch

"Good advice is always certain to be ignored, but that's no reason not to give it."
– Agatha Christie

I f severing ties was a mixed bag for me, it was even more so for my parents. On one hand, they reassured me repeatedly of their pride in my choice of alternate service and expressed their excitement about both my teaching assignment and its exotic location. They were a bit concerned about my safety, but I sensed mostly support. I was certainly doing the right thing, in their minds, they insisted. This was a very reassuring message to hear. It added to my own excitement and anticipation of a great adventure ahead.

On the other hand, both Mom and Dad had *lots* of advice for me. The range of their suggestions seemed limitless: how to conduct myself as a teacher and professional, how to relate to the mission community, how to prepare various basic meals, how to foster my spiritual growth, what to do if I got sick, how to fill leisure time, and how to avoid sexual and/or romantic disasters. My parents seemed to feel they had a *lot* to fit into the short time remaining before I left them for Africa.

While I understood their need to send me off well prepared, it didn't take long for me to tire of their well-meaning lectures and to – subtly as I could – deflect conversations that seemed headed in the direction of advice giving. I made a mental note that if I *were* to encounter any of the issues or obstacles they addressed, I'd better use caution in how much information I shared lest I subject myself to further uninvited rounds of parental warnings and directives, delivered via air mail.

Following this pattern consistently, two years later I caught them very much by surprise with an announcement of my serious interest in a girl I met in Africa – a young woman who would eventually become my wife. But, this is getting ahead of my story.

Psychologist Roger Gould refers to this period of life as *"Leaving the parents' world."* He suggests that young people typically move from depending upon their parents beliefs and support to increasingly making decisions and developing confidence in *their own* ability to care for themselves. He notes that they often report feeling "half-in, half-out of the family" as they wrestle with issues of independence and competence, learning to rely on non-family members.

I believe that is a very accurate description of my

reactions to Mom and Dad's advice-giving. I was absolutely ready to detach from my supportive family and to spread my wings. While externally projecting confidence, I was also privately battling self-doubt and ambivalence about how to proceed.

In spite of my resistance to parental influence, I don't mean to suggest that I was at odds with Mom and Dad: I carried a strong sense of their interest and affirmation. This was especially true of my relationship with my mother. She was a stay-at-home mom who doubled as the family psychologist. Mom had a gift of engaging with people in a warm and authentic manner. She was a good listener who effectively practiced and applied these skills with my older sister and me. There was no dodging her radar when something was awry. Mom had been a grammar school teacher before she and dad married, but she made an enthusiastic career of meeting needs in her home, church and neighborhood.

My dad was also concerned with our well being as a family and with our interests and activities as children growing up. He was clearly a product of the Great Depression, however. His first concern was work and being a good professional educator and provider. He was a middle school principal for most of my childhood. His school commitments and concerns were his number one priority. As a result, his faculty loved him, vying to stay with him whenever administrative reassignments were made in the school district. They may have had more of his attention than we did before he retired. When Dad wasn't on the job he still worked: tending a big garden, taking care of the yard and preparing lessons for the adult Sunday School class at church where he taught for many years. Dad didn't know how to play, and had trouble relaxing. He therefore wasn't very sympathetic to my requests for him to shoot baskets with me or to take me fishing. Still, as I became proficient in sports, dad evolved into an ardent fan, never missing a game – even for school meetings.

. . . .

My next step involved a stop in the Midwest. The Christian Service program required us participants to attend an orientation in the tiny central Kansas town of Hillsboro where the Mennonite Brethren Missions headquarters were located. We CS volunteers would then depart for our respective assignments in Africa, Central and South America directly from the orientation.

The first travel challenge of my adventure came in the form of a national airline strike that commenced just days before the scheduled departure date for Kansas. The only realistic travel option at that late hour was to take a train from Portland, Oregon, to Abilene, Kansas – the nearest stop to my Hillsboro destination. I therefore planned to head to the orientation from the Union Pacific railway station in Portland.

In the course of corresponding with CS headquarters, I was informed that a total of four volunteers would be assuming teaching assignments at the same location in the Congo, Africa. Two of the four in our group were an attractive, low-key, married couple from central California, Garry and Lois Schmidt. Both were recent graduates of Pacific College (PC), later renamed Fresno Pacific College, now Fresno Pacific University. The remaining two included a single fellow, Jim Becker, from Salem, Oregon, and me. Jim had attended PC for two years with the Schmidts before transferring to Seattle Pacific University from which he had just graduated. He and I were scheduled to be roommates in Africa.

I quickly followed up on this information. Jim's proximity as a fellow Oregonian was a plus. We visited by phone several times, exchanging packing tips and contact information. We arranged to meet and travel together by train to our Kansas orientation.

A final severing of home ties came in the form of a surprise announcement from my mother regarding my departure from the Portland train depot. She approached me about two days prior to my leaving and with dry-eyed resolve, informed me that she had come to a difficult decision. Mom indicated she had decided *not* to see me off on the train in Portland. She explained that she had given the matter a lot of thought and prayer and had determined that it was important for my father and me to make that final trip to the station together – just the two of us.

Dad and I had experienced a good deal of conflict in our relationship during my teen years and Mom let me know that she perceived this departure event as a turning point for the two of us. In essence, Dad would serve as the official parental launching representative. In retrospect, it was wise symbolism.

At first I was surprised and a little confused by my mother's announcement, but she assured me that she loved me deeply and that it was in the best interests of all of us. I accepted her decision with a hearty hug and a heavy heart.

This departure thing was becoming real. It seemed, however, adventure comes with a price tag.

John and Mom before departure, July 1966

5

The Departure

*"Some of us think holding on makes us strong; but
sometimes it is letting go."*
– Herman Hesse

We gathered in a small group in the old Union Pacific station in Portland. We stood there, awkwardly, the way families sometimes do before a member departs on a long trip, mostly watching and waiting and only intermittently addressing one another. My father and I faced my travel partner and Christian Service teammate, Jim, with his mother and father crowded closely on either side of him. My mother had stuck to her resolve to let this be a father-son experience and bid me a tearful goodbye at our doorstep in Eugene a couple of hours earlier.

As we stood there, Jim's mother kept the conversation alive, referencing his two older brothers, train travel, Kansas weather and other miscellaneous items.

My dad volunteered to Jim's father "the boys are doing a good thing in choosing alternate service." He made some other small talk and references to WWII service that I didn't follow very carefully. I was still in a daze from a spinning combination of thoughts and emotions: my dad's disclosures in the drive from Eugene, my anxiety about leaving familiar Oregon for two years in unfamiliar Africa, and my excitement about finally heading out on this undefined adventure.

The drive from Eugene to Portland had been an illuminating one for me. My father shared his observations and feelings about leaving for service with Mennonite Central Committee (MCC) some 27 years earlier, at the onset of World War II. He served as the Western Regional Director of Civilian Public Service units, which provided alternative service opportunities for conscientious objectors during the war. His departure, like mine on that cloudy afternoon in July 1966, had been prompted by the military draft. My unsavory encounter with *my* draft board was an echo of similar hassles in my father's era.

Many of my father's reflections – pacifist convictions, anxiety, uncertainty, determination, and sadness – contained new information for me. I don't remember my father *ever* sharing his feelings with me in that kind of detail prior to that drive. I savored the bonding experience as he clearly identified with my leaving home to do alternate service during wartime. I was flattered and a little overwhelmed by this unexpected sharing of "confidences" with me. Perhaps my mother was right, maybe it *was* a new beginning for us as father and son.

So, there we stood in the Portland train station. The noble neo-Elizabethan brick and timbered structure had once been a grand entrance to the City of Roses. By July of 1966, however, it was but a shabby ghost of a bygone era. Jim and I each had our two suitcases filled with clothes to last for two years of living abroad. In addition, Jim had a guitar case and a small bag with some cookies and a container of potato salad his mother had prepared for our journey. I carried a reel tape recorder, the current technology, which I intended to use to communicate with my parents from my post in "darkest Africa."

The dim Union Pacific station was crowded with others who, like us, were heading for the Midwest, but had been forced to take to the rails by the nationwide airline strike. We wondered how many of the 30 or so other young people expected in our Christian Service orientation would be voyaging to Kansas by train. We were the only ones coming from the Northwest.

Finally, the time arrived to board the train. Jim and I hugged our parents and lugged our bags up into the train car. It turned out that the train we boarded was the historic "Portland Rose" that once proudly traveled between Portland and Chicago starting in the 1930s. While the 44-seat coach we entered at one time boasted many services and amenities, by the time we boarded her she was but a relic, a fading antique.

The seats were worn, the prevailing color – soft, deep pink of "Madame Caroline Testout," the official rose of Portland – was faded; there was no air conditioning, and the windows were all open in spite of it being a gray, overcast afternoon. We quickly discovered that in the haste to accommodate the rush of diverted travelers, the train had no accompanying dining car. With the windows open on a muggy July day, diesel fumes and train noises only compounded the shabby conditions of the coach. It was thus with some foreboding that we waved goodbye to our family members and settled back as the train pulled out from the station.

Though our travel conditions were far from ideal, the afternoon and evening passed quickly and in relatively good spirits for our fellow train travelers and us. The train traversed along the scenic Columbia River Gorge until we reached the tiny Umatilla County town of Hinkle, where the UP tracks took a southeast turn, heading toward Nampa, Idaho.

This was the first opportunity Jim and I had really had to get acquainted with one another and we took full advantage of it. Starting with our recent preparations for travel and moving through divergent interests, frustration with college experiences, common resistance to teaching as a career goal, and touching on relationships – family and girl friends – we quickly discovered much common ground and the roots of a significant friendship.

Where were we headed in life? Neither of us had

a firm grip on that question as we rattled along the tracks. What we *could* agree upon was that we were launching into the big adult world, full speed ahead. At least we had company! Before we knew it, darkness had descended and we found ourselves still engrossed in conversation somewhere in southern Idaho, headed east.

At that point in our train journey things took a decided downturn. My parents had reassured me prior to departure that "all transcontinental trains have food service available," so I brought nothing with me to eat. It didn't take long for the two of us guys to finish off Jim's mother's chocolate chip cookies, and after determining that her potato salad had become rancid we were done with our on-board eating.

Forays into adjacent train cars confirmed our information at departure: no food service was available on this train! Tell *that* to two 22-year-old *hungry* fellows. We were not happy with our accommodations. We then decided to cut our losses and grab some sleep as we clacked and swayed along, curled and contorted on the worn train seats.

In the middle of the night, however, the mother of a wide-awake, hyperactive, little 3-year-old traveler broke out a new toy for him to play with. For well over an hour that little fellow ran up and down the aisles in our train car pulling his "clack-clack duck" behind him.

Jim and I speculated how quickly we might scoop

up the obnoxious child and fling him out the window of the coach. Clearly, his mother was paying him no heed. We decided that *purposeful homicide* was not really compatible with our pacifist beliefs, and besides, it would be hard to confess that, however justified, we had just taken a life on the way to our Christian Service orientation.

Two notable occurrences animated the remainder of that endless night on the train. One, was a jarring stop at Green River, Wyoming, which woke us up fully though only briefly. The abrupt stop nearly ejected us from our seats, but we quickly fell, not drifted back to sleep. The second was a stop at the break of dawn in Cheyenne for breakfast. Jim and I were among the first to leap off the train following our porter's announcement that we would have a 45-minute stop for food.

Did someone say *"food stop?"*

We rushed to the nearest tiny café just off the tracks and adjacent to the train station. I believe that *very place* must surely be the *original source* of the expression "greasy spoon." Our fried eggs had rivulets of butter rolling off of the blackened edges and the burned toast was similarly soaked in the stuff. Famished, we gobbled it all down and rushed back to our train car, full but not just a little nauseous.

As the new day dawned and the Portland Rose headed onto the prairie from Denver, a dramatic, panoramic vista opened up to us. This was my first view of the Great Plains and I was genuinely amazed at the endless grasslands stretching out to the horizon on both sides of the tracks. It felt like my whole world was opening up. Familiar boundaries could no longer contain my life. It was exhilarating.

By mid afternoon we made our final stop at our destination of Abilene, Kansas. This historic cattle town and former residence of Wild Bill Hickok was where we took leave of our railed transport. Bags stacked on the platform, we looked for our ride to Hillsboro and our orientation. The time had arrived to learn what we had signed on for and to meet our fellow Christian Service colleagues.

6
The Next Step...Orientation

"There should be less talk. A preaching point is not a meeting point."
– Mother Teresa of Calcutta

Jim and I stood quietly on the train platform and surveyed our surroundings. It was overcast, a humid Friday afternoon in early July. I believe this was the first time in my life that I had been anywhere with no mountains or even large hills in sight. Everything was laid out in straight lines: fences, roads, and crops. Even the cattle walked in lines, or so it seemed. Perhaps this was what characterized Midwest culture I had only heard about previously – order, simplicity, structure, and predictability.

A slender, white-haired man waved and approached us with a welcoming smile. Frank Klaassen, a retiree who worked with the Mennonite Brethren Missions and Services, was there at the station to meet us.

"John and Jim?" he quizzed in a friendly, low-key greeting.

We loaded our bags into the back of his station wagon. Mr. Klaassen had a son, David, who would join us as a Christian Service teacher in the Congo just a year later. We did not know that then, however, as we chatted about our forgettable train ride from Oregon and informally introduced ourselves during the hour's drive south to Hillsboro.

As we exited the car and headed for the dorm rooms where we were to be housed for the week, we heard a loud, raspy staccato sound all around us in the dense afternoon air. We were told that the penetrating noise was the "17-year cicadas" plying their mating melody at full volume. I can only imagine that at age 22, we hoped our future sex lives would be more generously paced than that being modeled by these obnoxious insects.

We stayed in the new dorms at Tabor College, a small Christian liberal arts institution sponsored by the Mennonite Brethren denomination. As we began to meet our fellow orientation peers, it became clear that most of the 33 "orientees" had recently graduated from either Tabor or its sister school, Pacific College, in Fresno, California. There were eight couples in the group. The attendees were gathered from four states and four Canadian provinces, but nearly half came from California. Twenty-four of our group members were going into Christian Service teaching assignments.

July 1966 Christian Service Orientation;
Jim front left, John middle back

Because of so many familiar denominational and educational connections, most of my fellow volunteers eagerly launched into getting acquainted with one another by identifying common experiences, histories and friends. I felt like a duck out of water. I concede I *was* an Oregon Duck after all, but at this moment, I just felt like a *dumb duck!* I was glad to have had some conversations with Jim on the train, however brief, about his Pacific College experiences, and about Mennonites in general. I could thus at least marginally track the interaction going on around me.

I had never, however, prior to that experience,

played the *"Menno name game."* This interactive exchange involves identifying ones parents' families, mother's maiden name, and so on to trace possible relational connections. It was apparently a common strategy for building relationships among Mennonites. It still is, some 40+ years later, though expanding diversity among the faithful has eroded its value and therefore, the practice itself.

My problem was that I didn't know a "Mennonite name" from any other German-sounding name. I had only just joined my home MB church two years earlier as a charter member, and I knew little about the denomination or my ethnic heritage. Few Mennonites lived in my hometown. I had not ever attached any particular significance to my grandparents' family names, and therefore had no usable genealogical vocabulary. Besides, my father's background was not from Mennonite Brethren roots, but what was known then as the General Conference Mennonite denomination. To top it all off, my mother was not a so-called "ethnic Mennonite." Her family origins were from England and Scotland, not Poland or South Russia. That fact proved to be a conversation stopper in this particular get-acquainted process.

In fairness, it should be noted, however, that the experience of getting acquainted and building relationships at this event was very different for some of my peers than what I have described. For example, Helen Claassen of Hillsboro, KS, and Harold Ens of Dinuba,

CA, ended up on the same team headed for a teaching assignment in Cali, Colombia. They fell in love, were eventually married and served for a number of years as career Mennonite Brethren Missions/Services (MBMS) missionaries. The Menno name game paid off well for them.

Harold Ens later became the head of MBMS. In a real twist of fate, the Ens' eventually had a daughter, Carmen, and I had a daughter, Mindy, who, 26 years after our meeting at this orientation event, would enroll in Fresno Pacific College, become roommates and best friends. Our lives – the Ens' and mine – would intersect once again. Garry and Lois Schmidt from Bakersfield, the couple who accompanied Jim and me to our assignment in TASOK, Congo eventually had a daughter, Heidi, who would also join Carmen and Mindy as roommates and close friends at college. Who could ever have predicted such outcomes when we all met for the first time those many years ago?

These first encounters partially answered the "who" of my orientation to Christian Service, but not the "what." I was about to receive what we later light-heartedly described as a spiritual force-feeding.

As an orientation for young adults headed for overseas teaching assignments, our Christian Service event was a pretty *impractical* experience. There were more hours of one-way teaching/preaching than I, for one, had ever been exposed to in a single week.

Some meaningful points surfaced in each of the

sessions, to be sure. For example, one speaker stressed the need for us to be flexible in our expectations and reactions to others in our new settings; another emphasized the value of appreciating differences and showing respect, versus imposing our judgments and practices on people from other traditions and cultures. A local pastor delivered articulate sermons that illuminated appropriate attitudes toward service. These were helpful and sensitive reflections that inspired and challenged us.

For the most part, however, our orientation consisted of too many sermons, too many monologues and too little practical preparation for service. Suggestions for improvement offered by my fellow attendees were captured in the week's final summary documents. They echo my sentiments.

The following observations were included: "Less time should be given to men who felt they should preach at us..."

"I would like to have had more instruction on the changing position of a missionary, but instead received a "missionary indoctrination."

"More time should be devoted to small discussion groups wrestling with practical problems we will face on the field."

"We were treated as missionaries too often...we need to integrate Christianity and teaching." (Source: *Impact: the Christian Service newsletter,* 2/2, July-August 1966, p. 15)

It's entirely possible that the lack of specificity in our orientation actually served to open the door for the exercise of our creative instincts. At least, that's what happened next.

7

Europe Through the Back Door

"All journeys have secret destinations of which the traveler is unaware."

– Martin Buber

P lied with spiritual inspiration, challenged to identify with the purposes of MBMS and primed with enthusiasm for overseas adventure by our new teammates/friends, our orientation was complete. The four of us assigned to teach in the American School of Kinshasa (TASOK), Democratic Republic of the Congo, boarded a van that took us from Hillsboro to the airport in Wichita, Kansas.

The next steps in our Christian Service journey were clearly defined: flight schedule, accommodations, agenda. However, as poet Robert Burns once noted, "The best laid plans of mice and men often go awry." No matter how carefully something may be planned, "stuff" happens, *especially* when you are youthful, naive, fearless young adults, eager for adventure.

While the airline strike had not been fully settled during our orientation week, we were able to secure routing from Wichita to New York on air carriers that were still flying. Then, after a three-day stay we were scheduled to continue on a marathon 23-hour Pan Am flight from NY to Kinshasa, Congo, our final destination.

Curiously – to us then and to me now, decades later – the Director of Christian Service wanted us to "see the United Nations" before proceeding from the Big Apple to our Africa assignment. Did that mean merely standing in front of the UN building, looking? Were we supposed to interview someone there: for what purpose? Collect brochures? Whatever function this "inspired" routing was designed to fulfill, it was then, and remains today, a complete mystery to us four compliant volunteers heading for Africa.

Our small cohort on this voyage included Jim and me plus traveling companions and Christian Service colleagues, Garry and Lois Schmidt. The teaching assignments of us four fresh college grads had been clarified during our orientation in Hillsboro. Garry was scheduled to teach junior and senior high history courses and junior high P.E; Lois was assigned to teach second grade; Jim's assignment was English, journalism and speech instruction at the high school level. I had been assigned to teach 8th and 9th grade science, biology and high school P.E.

TASOK, where we were headed, was an English-speaking school with an American curriculum established by missionaries and diplomats serving in the Congo in the early 1960s following that African country's independence. While mostly an American dependents' school, by 1966 TASOK had grown to nearly 400 students (K – 12), boosted by numbers of children from English-speaking families of business and military attachés from many different countries. The school was very international in culture, *except for the teaching staff*, which was predominantly white, American, and directly or indirectly affiliated with missionary organizations. We four volunteers fit that profile to a "T."

Garry was the only one of our little group who had ever previously traveled abroad, though his experiences were limited to voyaging to and from India with his parents as a young child. For all practical purposes we could thus be accurately classified as a group of very novice travelers. That status didn't limit our adventuresome spirit, however.

As we met together for lunch in New York City, following our meaningless visit to the UN, we reflected on the long trip before us. "It's sure a shame that we are going *all that way* and will miss seeing Europe. I've never been to Europe." None of us had. After a brief reflective pause, in a sudden flash of inspiration, Garry volunteered, "You know what? It might be possible to exchange our tickets for a stop in Europe without it costing us anything extra."

"Let's check it out!" was the consensus of our group. We left our café and headed for 5th Avenue, the location of numerous airline agencies. Jim and I started down the street in one direction and Garry and Lois set out in the other, stopping in one airline office after another. It was mid-July, the height of the travel season and each query produced the same result: "Four seats to Europe in the next two days? Impossible."

After an hour or more we finally met one another at an agreed-upon street corner and determined we had covered all the nearby offices, with no success. We were very disappointed but not willing to let go of the idea quite yet.

As we waited for the light to change, I turned to a tall lady in her mid-30s, standing beside us and asked, "Do you know of any other airline offices nearby? We have contacted every office on this street with no luck." She replied with a few questions of her own, quizzing us about what we were trying to accomplish.

As we explained our quest, a strange look spread across the lady's face.

"You're in luck," she said with a smile. "Coincidentally, I happen to work for a *travel agency* and my boss just might be able to assist you. Follow me."

Not having any other plan, we complied.

The self-identified travel clerk led us two or three blocks down the main street and then turned into a narrow alley. A block or so later we came to a dingy, old multi-story building. We entered a weathered back door, scaled a dark stairway and followed our mystery lady to the third floor of the building. Down each dimly lit hallway were a series of glass doors with gold leaf lettering. We four adventurers were getting increasingly nervous about the direction this contact had taken us. Was this our own special angel, or a street-wise lady setting us up for a mugging?

"Garry, should we be doing this?" Lois asked in a quavering, whispered voice.

Before he had a chance to answer, "We're here!" our guide proclaimed. The lettering on the door indicated it was indeed a travel agency, "Global Travels" or some such moniker.

The cheerful clerk introduced us to her boss and we quickly explained what we'd like to accomplish. "Let's see what we can do," offered the balding, middle-aged Jewish travel agent, in a hopeful tone. As we sat in the hard-backed chairs facing his desk, he then proceeded to make a series of phone calls: "Maury, this is Sol. I need a favor. That's right, four air tickets in the next two days to somewhere in Europe, a city from which I can make connections to Africa."

Astonishingly, in the end, our enterprising travel agent was successful. He exchanged our tickets straight across for a flight to Milan, Italy, with a connecting flight to Rome, all on Alitalia Air. The departure was the very next day. He managed to give us three days in that magical city and to make on-going connections to Kinshasa, on the same airline.

A chance encounter on a New York street corner had resulted in a new opportunity of our own making. We were very pleased with ourselves. What enterprising young adults we were turning out to be! Where would we stay and what would we do once we arrived in Italy? We didn't have a clue. But it's dealing with unknowns that transform experiences into adventures, as we were about to find out.

8

Viva Roma

*"Me thinks I would not die quite happy without having
seen something of Rome..."*
– Sir Walter Scott

Our 13-hour flight to Milan was a unique experience in itself. We apparently *did* secure the last
four tickets, as the plane was packed. The airline seat
rows were so close together that my long legs were
jammed tight against the seat in front. I couldn't move.
Lois and Garry sat immediately in front of Jim and me
and shared in the discomfort. Lois was unable to recline
her seat back at all – my compressed knees blocked any
movement. As grimly uncomfortable as it was, I was
grateful just to *have* a seat. We all were.

We passed some of the time by playing Hearts with
the Schmidts draped over the back of their seats. The
flight was an unanticipated cross-cultural experience.
The in-flight movie was in Italian, pasta and wine were

served at mealtime. As the long voyage ended and the aircraft at last touched down on Italian soil, the entire plane broke into song, *in Italian*, presumably the national anthem.

Viva Milano!

After an unremarkable layover of several boring hours, mostly spent in the airport lounge, we again boarded a plane for the final hour's flight to our Italian destination.

Viva Roma!

Travel mates Lois, Garry & Jim deplane in Italy

It was well after dark when we arrived at Rome's Leonardo da Vinci-Fiumicino Airport, and by the time we retrieved our luggage, it was nearing midnight. As we approached the tourist assistance window, we could see the sleepy agent was closing up shop. We begged the bleary-eyed lady to help us, explaining that with our last minute change of plans we had been unable to make any arrangements for a place to stay in Rome.

In truth, we had not even thought of lodging until we landed. Reluctantly, but kindly the lady reopened her window and started making phone calls.

After several unsuccessful attempts to locate a place for us to stay, the agent called us over. Employing her strong Italian accent, she explained "Roma ees piena – full of turisti." We had *only one option*. She had managed to locate a "pensione" – bed and breakfast hotel – that was willing to put the four of us up for that first night, on cots in their dining area. The drawback was that we'd have to get up at 6 AM sharp so the staff could prepare the continental breakfast for hotel guests. The following two nights they had rooms available for us.

"We'll take it!" we chorused in unison.

The taxi ride to the pensione was yet another cross-cultural experience, in non-communication. We spoke no Italian. The taxi driver spoke no English. None of us knew how many Italian lire there were to a dollar, let alone how to decipher whatever numbers the driver was citing. I'd wager it was the quartet of us unprepared, young Americans that got the short end of things that night. At least we had made it to Europe! Our first step onto the bridge of cross-cultural "perspective transformation," a term coined by psychologist Jack Mezirow, had taken place with our arrival in Rome. But we were not aware of the significance of that momentous step at the time. We were simply four exhausted travelers. We crashed on our cots in the pensione dining room for a pitiful few hours of sleep before being rousted awake by our Italian hosts.

Our adventures in Rome seem but a blur in retrospect. I do clearly recall that one of the first things we did was to find a Western Union office in order to send an ill-fated telegram to the American School in Kinshasa, indicating that we would be arriving there at a different time and on a different airline than originally scheduled.

Jim reminded me years later that our first real meal in Rome consisted of chicken and potatoes completely soaked in grease. Subsequent to that unique culinary experience, he recalls our tour of Rome being punctuated by a continual search for bathrooms due to a bad case of intestinal distress. It is true that we nearly ran from place to place in an attempt to squeeze as much sightseeing as possible into our limited available time.

We sampled the famous Italian gelato and bought warm cokes from street vendors. The Coliseum, Pantheon, Trevi Fountain, and St. Peter's Basilica & Square – we covered all the major tourist attractions in Rome at an exhausting pace only those in their early

20s can accomplish. We moved quickly. At times that included making good use of Rome's public restrooms.

At the Trevi Fountain, site of the classic 1954 song and movie, *"Three Coins in a Fountain"*, a young woman called my name from across the famous water feature. It took several tries before she got my attention. "Someone calling out *my* name *in Rome*? I can't be hearing this," I thought.

The voice came from a vacationing former classmate from the University of Oregon; a girl I sat next to in Shakespeare class. We chatted briefly, exchanging first impressions and discoveries from our Rome adventures thus far. How nice to have a witness on my first stop to the future. My three travel companions were duly impressed. All the way to Europe and *recognized!* That was good for the ego. Who needed coins in the fountain for luck?

Tired, but proud of ourselves for transforming a potentially long, boring direct flight to Africa into an unexpected adventure in Europe, after three days we boarded our Alitalia flight headed for Kinshasa.

"How could things get more exciting than this?" we asked ourselves.

Little could we have imagined what awaited us at our destination.

9

Surprising Africa

"All I know is that every time I go to Africa I am shaken to my core."
– Stephen Lewis

T he seven-hour flight from Rome to Kinshasa was paradoxically more relaxed and at the same time, more stimulating than our previous transcontinental experience on Alitalia Air. The plane was less than half full, for one thing, so it was possible to actually raise armrests, stretch out and sleep on empty rows. I say it was possible, but we four young American travelers were far too excited to do any sleeping on that flight, anticipating our arrival in Africa. We spent the long hours visiting, humming along with Jim's guitar playing, writing post cards to our families, leafing through dog-eared airline magazines and just speculating about what we would find at the end of our flight.

We hoped that there would be representatives from

TASOK at the airport eager to help us get through customs, whatever that entailed, and to transport us to our residences, whatever and wherever they were. It dawned on us that seven flight hours from our departure would have us arriving in Kinshasa sometime after midnight, 12:30 AM to be specific.

"I hope they don't mind staying up late. We probably won't see much of Kinshasa in the middle of the night."

The latter observation proved to be quite accurate.

As our plane made a final banking turn we all found a window seat and pressed our faces to the glass to get our first glimpse of the city of five million plus inhabitants. What we saw was...*nothing*. The plane completed its half circle, and at last two parallel lines of purple airport landing lights stretched out before us. Surrounding the lights? Night. Blackness. An intimation of things to come?

The plane touched down, the interior lights were turned fully on and a strongly accented announcement crackled on the intercom in three languages – Italian, French and English. "Ladies and gentlemen, you have just landed at the Ndjili Airport in Kinshasa, Democratic Republic of the Congo. Please do not move about before the seat-belt sign is extinguished. Thank you for flying Alitalia Air."

Our aircraft came to a full stop, sleepy passengers stirred throughout, overhead bins were opened and conversations buzzed here and there in various languages. Our team of four gathered our carry-on pieces and headed for the door of the plane.

As we debarked down the stairs to the tarmac, we received our first impression of Africa. The image was one of stepping into some sort of giant pungent sauna. Emotionally, it felt like something more mystical; like entering an alternate dimension or crossing a portal into a new world. In contrast to the cool, air-conditioned plane interior, the night air was very warm and humid, so much so that it felt hard to breathe at first. The dense air carried a strange mixture of unfamiliar scents, a combination of odors: fuel oil, decayed plants, human waste, and who knows what else.

We expressed surprise to one another at how warm it was at that late hour of the night, as we walked the hundred yards or so from the plane to the dimly lit two-story airport terminal building. A sleepy-looking airport worker in a frayed, baggy jump suit pointed us toward an open door in the airport terminal.

Entering the Ndjili Airport terminal building provided yet another new assault to our senses. The building itself could best be described as dirty yellow in color, with chipped tile floors, rows of torn, attached seats scattered here and there and pockmarked cement walls. We later were informed that these wall chips were defects caused by bullets having been sprayed throughout the interior of the building from gun battles both during independence in 1960 and again four years later – just two years prior to our arrival – during a rebel uprising.

The terminal was dirty and dimly lit with intermittent florescent bulbs located high in the ceiling above us and occasionally placed on the side walls. Since bulbs were intermittently missing or burned out, the randomness of light sources produced a strange effect: irregular shadows and dream-like illumination.

As we entered the terminal, however, a most startling and sinus-impacting experience greeted us. The strong and pervasive odor of urine penetrated the facility. Apparently, hygiene standards and bladder relief practices were different in Africa. At that moment I was *very* thankful I had used the facilities in the plane prior to landing, though the terminal apparently *did* offer unlimited opportunities for relief.

We followed the short line of passengers who had deplaned with us. Most of the small number of adults was African, though there were three or four Europeans in addition to the four of us Americans. The line wound its way through the downstairs terminal area to a large room where, after a short delay, our baggage was delivered, by hand, off of a rickety cart. It was a relief to discover that all of our luggage had arrived in Africa at the same time as we.

Each of the passengers slid their luggage along a low aluminum counter and one by one, passed through customs, administered by similarly clad officials. Each of the agents was attired in a white shirt, dark slacks and wearing an official hat that read, *"Douane"* in French. We did not know what this meant or what was happening. Things had been much more casual in the Rome airport.

Most of the passengers in front of us passed quickly by the customs agents and we could see and hear them warmly greeting their family or friends as they exited the area with their bags. Our anxious glances toward the exit door did not locate *anyone* looking in our direction or waiting for *us*. Each passenger in line was questioned. A few were asked to open their bags. We could not understand either the questions or the answers, but we saw the agents dramatically place a chalk check mark on each bag that was passed.

Finally, it was our quartet's turn to be checked. While not understanding the questions posed to us in French, we dutifully opened each of our bags when motioned to do so. The Congolese custom agents took their time looking through our luggage. They seemed entertained as they pulled out and examined various items, lifting them up and turning them slowly over. What should we make of this action? Did we look like smugglers? What were they looking for?

One agent reached for the tape recorder held by a strap slung around my neck. He pulled one direction voicing loud, annoyed declarations in French. I pulled back, confused and alarmed at this seeming attempt to snatch my precious machine.

As we grappled with my recorder, a little man with an Alitalia Air monogram on his shirt came striding up. He addressed the four of us in broken English, "You let me help here! Step back."

After several animated exchanges in French with

my customs agent, the conversational tone changed. The Alitalia agent handed something to the customs man. The latter then turned to us and in exaggerated slow motion, placed a chalk check mark on each of our bags, including my tape recorder. He then slowly and somberly turned on his heel and drifted away.

The Alitalia agent faced us and with smiling eyes, explained that he had had to give up a perfectly good ballpoint pen, but that he and the customs fellow were now "good friends." We were free to leave.

We thanked him profusely. He just laughed.

This first official contact with Congolese immediately exposed our cultural and linguistic vulnerability. Students of culture would identify this as our first real "disorienting dilemma." That is, we were confronted with new and novel circumstances that challenged our sense of confidence, unseating our previous securities. "Living abroad might be more difficult than we thought" was the silent message passed in anxious glances to one another.

Little did we know how much more difficult it would be.

10

A Little Bit of Help

"It is surmounting difficulties that makes heroes."
– Louis Pasteur

S haken, but greatly relieved at making it past our initial African encounter, we dragged our luggage through the exit door and out to the dark exterior of the terminal. Where were our greeters? What were we supposed to do now? How could we even ask for help, let alone directions, speaking no French?

A dirty old bus, labeled "Air Congo" was idling nearby and several of the African passengers from our plane were standing by the door. We motioned to them in a questioning tone, "Bus to Kinshasa?" They nodded.

We dragged our bags into the bus and in a few minutes, belching diesel smoke, it chugged off into the night. "Now what?" we thought. We were almost too tired and overwhelmed to speak to one another as we silently sat on that uncomfortable bus, wondering where it would take us.

The ride from the airport was dark and noisy from the aged bus' diesel engine. Every so often, through the darkness we would see some low buildings and a small fire with dim figures seated nearby. Mostly it was just a bumpy, smelly ride through "darkest Africa," giving us yet additional new meaning to the hackneyed expression.

Midnight ride on a bus like this

After a half hour or so, the bus came to a full stop and an African man dressed in a business suit, the same fellow who had initially motioned for us to get on the bus, exited with his bags. We did not know what to do. "Kinshasa?" we asked the non-responsive driver. We four neophytes clambered out of the bus along with all of our luggage. We were feeling very young, very white and very out of place. The bus was stopped in front of a dark building. There were no lights anywhere to be seen. We were in the dark in more ways than one.

"Where are we, anyhow?"

The businessman, who had started off into the night, turned and walked quickly back toward us shaking his head, "no" as he did so.

"Kinshasa n'est pas ici," he said in carefully articulated French, motioning for us to get back on board the bus. We did, grateful for his helpful intervention. Who knows *what* we would have done had we remained stranded in the middle of nowhere in the middle of the night.

The bus continued on its way and about twenty minutes later, we approached what appeared to be the downtown area.

John, gesturing out the window: *"Kinshasa?"* Bus driver: *"Oui."*

We approached an area where there were a number of businesses with lighted signs and some multi-story apartment buildings with exterior lights. On what appeared to be a main avenue, there were actually streetlights burning. The bus stopped in front of a multi story corner building with a sign reading, *"Memling Hotel"* on the front marquee.

As we drew near this terminal point for the airport bus, we noticed that many of the nearby structures had someone – a guard? – lying or sleeping on cardboard in front of the doorway. Some of the figures were awake with a small warming fire burning at their feet. All of the doorway dwellers had either a machete or a metal spear next to them.

Complying with the driver's hand motions, we exited the bus, as did the remaining passengers. They quickly headed off into the urban night, presumably for home. We stacked our luggage in a small pile in front of the hotel entrance.

At that point, Garry had a revelation.

"Hey, guys. I just remembered that I have a telephone number that someone gave me for the American Baptist Mission. Let's try to call for help."

"Wait with the luggage," he told Lois over his shoulder, as the three of us brave guys headed off into the hotel lobby.

By that time, it was about 1:45 AM.

What happened next was a nearly inexplicable set of exchanges, pantomimed, between the three of us fellows and the hotel's bleary-eyed night clerk. In the end, the man at the front desk reluctantly gave us permission to use the hotel's phone. Garry dug out the mission number and dialed.

After a long delay, miracle-of-miracles, someone actually answered the phone! It was the sleepy, unfocused 15-year-old daughter of the mission's director. Young, inexperienced and only half-awake, she was ill-prepared to serve as our rescuer on this occasion. What ill fortune to reach her of all people. After Garry spilled out our tale of woe, the groggy adolescent proceeded to

offer him a series of mumbled directions to their location. Then, she did the unbelievable: she abruptly hung
up!

What made this a particularly absurd and distressing response was that Kinshasa had no street signs and
we had no local currency or means of transportation to
the location of the Baptist compound, some miles away.
Even if we had had some money the streets were deserted of taxis.

Our pantomimed appeals to the desk clerk failed.
The annoyed fellow would not let Garry use the phone
a second time to call our hoped-for rescuer back.

Now what?

As we stood there, not knowing what to think or do
next, a high-pitched voice wailed from outside the front
of the hotel, "Gaaaarrrryyy!"

We rushed outside to see Lois, clutching our bags,
surrounded by a ragged circle of African men, most
likely night watchmen who had drifted over from
nearby businesses. They were clearly more curious
than threatening. Lois was terrified, however.

"Why did you leave me *alone* out here?" she exclaimed.

Why did we, indeed?

As we stood there, speechless in the midst of the
small circle of attendant Africans, a beat-up old VW
Beatle came chugging up to the curb. Out popped our
little Alitalia Air agent from the airport.

"I thought you might need help," he chuckled,
"How you say…by telepathy?" pointing to his head.

We explained what had happened, and he listened with an attentive but amused expression on his face. Since it was after 2 AM by then, he proposed that we come with him and stay at his flat for the rest of the night. It was just around the corner.

It took several trips with our rescuer's VW to transport our luggage around the block. We carried the bags up a flight of stairs to his second floor apartment. Garry and Lois slept in a spare bedroom and Jim and I gratefully spent our first night in Africa sleeping on the living room couch and chairs of the Alitalia agent's Kinshasa apartment.

Alitalia agent Angelo was our hero that night, for sure! He seemed more like a guardian angel, aptly named, *Angelo*.

What a Congo welcome that turned out to be! Our last thought before falling into a coma-like sleep: "What's clear is that we are in WAY over our heads! We're not in Kansas anymore, Toto."

11
A Delayed Welcome

"Beginnings are always messy."
– John Galsworthy

Morning comes abruptly at 6:15 AM in Kinshasa. Since the Congo is located on the equator, both dawn and sunset are predictable events that occur almost suddenly at twelve-hour intervals. Perhaps our previous night's experience should have clued us to how rapidly change happens in this setting. Our personal transformations were on a different time schedule, however. We four new arrivals to Africa were anything but ready to awake at that early hour, after only slightly more than four hours at our various sleep stations.

Nevertheless, the Congo dawn waits for no one and the sunlight streaming into the Alitalia agent's apartment roused us soon after daybreak. That, and the agent's breakfast preparations in his tiny kitchen area adjacent to where we slept.

By the time Jim and I were fully awake, he, curled up on a couch and me, stretched across several chairs in the living room, Angelo had already made a trip out to a nearby bakery for fresh bread. Garry and Lois emerged from his guest bedroom, as our host served up breakfast consisting of strong coffee, fresh bread and a variety of tropical fruit that was as wonderful as it was unfamiliar: mangos, sliced papaya, and fresh pineapple. Angelo explained that he was able to purchase fresh fruit from vendors who stopped by the apartment building several times a week.

We were impressed.

Frankly, we were also a bit distracted by the presence of several small lizards hanging above us on the walls and ceilings. Angelo explained that they were useful roommates, adept at catching mosquitoes, roaches and other undesirable insects and that their presence was just part of living in Africa.

There were a lot of things to get used to about living in Africa.

After breakfast, we followed our host down the stairs, out the door of his building and around the corner to the main street of Kinshasa. There was already a good deal of activity on the main street – taxis, buses, cars, vendors and pedestrians – even though it was early, barely 8:30 AM. We walked two blocks, wide-eyed and in a daze at the unfamiliar sights, sounds and smells that filled our senses.

One quick and obvious lesson from urban Kinshasa: whenever the odor of urine became especially strong, one could safely conclude a bus stop was nearby.

After a short walk, we came to a building with the sign *"Menno Travel Service"* posted on the front. Angelo explained that this was the main English-speaking travel agency in Kinshasa so he thought he'd deliver us there. "Menno Travel" in Africa? It was reassuring to see a familiar name.

We walked into the offices of the travel agency and the startled director, Rolin Reinheimer, immediately came forward to greet us – in American English. We introduced ourselves as the new TASOK teachers and his first words were: "What are you doing here *now?* You're not expected for several weeks yet."

We explained that we had made some changes in our travel itinerary and that we had sent a telegram en route from Rome to Kinshasa, but no one had been at the airport the night before to meet us. We pointed to Alitalia agent Angelo as our hero who had rescued us in the middle of the night.

Menno Travel Director Reinheimer explained that their agency made virtually *all* the airport runs for new English-speaking arrivals and that he had never received any *original* arrival notice for us, let alone an updating telegram from Rome.

We discovered later, typical of African cultural practices, although our telegram was received at the Kinshasa Post Office the *same day* it was sent, it ended up being placed in the TASOK mailbox three weeks *after* our unexpected arrival.

A VW Kombi was brought around to the front of the Menno Travel building to take us back to Angelo's apartment. There we loaded our bags and said our grateful goodbyes to this kind and generous man. Mr. Reinheimer then drove us down the broad, modern streets of downtown Kinshasa. The boulevards were impressive and in contrast with the empty streets the night before, there was lots of traffic.

After a half-mile or so we turned onto a side street and pulled into the Union Mission House (UMH) parking lot. We were told that this was a guesthouse for visiting missionaries. It was there our Menno Travel escort assumed we would be temporarily housed until the TASOK people could have time to prepare a place for us to stay.

It was a little troubling to discover that we were unexpected. We wondered how communication could have gotten so messed up and at our expense, no less. Our orientation hadn't prepared us for *this* contingency! Our sense of security and of trust in leaders who had sent us to the other side of the world without proper planning or notice were not strengthened by the developments we had experienced thus far.

Those were our sentiments at the time. Many years and travel experiences later, I have come to conclude that travel to and within Africa is more often accompanied by surprises than by uneventful predictability. Thus, our arrival experiences were probably not as unique as we thought them to be at the time.

As we pulled into the parking lot, a tall Caucasian man in his 40s waved at our driver and then came rushing across the street from in front of a building that had big signs reading "LECO" (Librairie Evangelique au Congo) across the front. After expressing a hello to Reinheimer, he asked if we were by chance new teachers for TASOK.

As we stepped out of the bus, he warmly greeted each of us, introducing himself as Larry Rempel, the Director of LECO, a printing house for Protestant churches. Rempel also served as the Secretary of the TASOK School Board. He exclaimed that it was a real surprise to see us there and that he would call the school's director/principal right away, but *first* we needed to join him and his family for the noon meal at their home across the street.

Larry Rempel's enthusiastic greeting and warm invitation flattered us. Finally, *someone* had legitimated our being there! What a relief. We unloaded our bags and cheerfully followed him across the street through his neatly groomed yard, to his comfortably functional whitewashed house.

The Rempels had been in the Congo for over twenty years, as builders – schools, hospitals, and churches – and more recently as administrators of the country's Protestant printing press. They had two daughters, Beverly, a college junior visiting them for the summer from the states, and Betty Jean, a high school senior at TASOK. Larry and his wife, Alvera, were among the first white missionaries to return to the Congo after independence and they had been instrumental in establishing TASOK so that their daughters and the children of other returning missionaries could join them and attend school nearby.

Our conversation at the table mostly consisted of get-acquainted small talk – where we were from, what subjects we planned to teach, and a bit about our adventures in arriving unannounced in the middle of the night. The two Rempel girls served us.

When the table conversation turned to matters of the school we four future teachers particularly took note. The new TASOK facility was currently under construction and not likely to be completed by the time classes would begin in the fall. The start of school would reportedly be even more chaotic than usual as some sort of double sessions would be required.

At one point in the conversation, fired up with 22-year-old idealism and hoping to impress our hosts, I volunteered, "We were told that previous Christian Service teachers at TASOK inappropriately crossed boundaries by actually *dating* students!" I denounced this practice and declared that we, the current crop, could certainly be expected to conduct ourselves in a more professional manner.

I don't think the Rempels knew what to say in response to my declaration at the time. I actually don't remember them saying anything at all. What I *do* painfully recall, however, is the number of times over the years that my then-future mother-in-law, Alvera Rempel, recalled those over-the-top statements offered in this first meeting. They proved to be about as naïve as they were ironic, since I would end up being the only one of our group to do the very thing I denounced. Recalling this first encounter some 45 years later, I'm grateful that since the beginning BJ has been more amused than put off at my ability to "insert foot in mouth."

After lunch, Larry Rempel drove us to a gated compound of several houses, leased by the American School for their teachers. Our principal and the school's director, Orv Wiebe, lived there with his wife, Ruby, and their two young daughters. Garry and Lois were scheduled to live in one of the houses in this compound. They quickly set about moving in. Jim and I were scheduled to live in apartments located some distance away, adjacent to the new TASOK school site. Our apartments were still under construction, however, so we were temporarily housed in another of the compound's homes, next to that of Gary and Lois. The rest of the teachers were not expected to arrive for several weeks.

Jim and I unpacked our bags and made our beds as darkness fell. We were carefully advised to be sure to lock all of our doors and to see that our cameras and electronics, such as my tape recorder, were locked away securely. Placing our socks and underwear in a chest of drawers, Jim and I marveled at how dangerous things seemed in our new locale. We had a gated compound, a night watchman, metal bars on all our windows, locks on the outside and bedroom doors and a lock on our closet. How were we *ever* going to get used to this? How often were homes actually broken into, we wondered. Were people injured or killed?

Our first Congo residence

Living in Africa seemed more than a little threatening.

At that point in our conversation, I found another pair of socks and reopened a drawer I had previously accessed. Sitting on top of my undershorts, feelers busily taking me in, was the biggest brown cockroach I had ever seen! It was a good three or four inches long.

"Eeeeekkk!" I screamed like a little girl.

Jim yelled as well, startled by my outburst. Once

we both finally landed, we diligently searched in vain for the phantom bug, shoes in hand poised to smack it. The cockroach had vanished.

Shaken by our experience, that night we used up two entire tubes of bug repellent, making chemical circles around our beds. Fearful from dinner hour stories of malaria, we also sprayed the room, emptying an entire can of bug spray. As we coughed and pulled our sheets up to retire for the night, I remember saying to Jim, "This is just our first night. How are we *ever* going to make it for *two years?*"

12

Entering a New World

*"The voyage of discovery is not in seeking new landscapes
but in having new eyes."*
– Marcel Proust

O ur first morning in our new home started with
a breakfast consisting of bread, jam, cheese, papaya and coffee at the nearby residence of the Wiebes.
We four novice teachers sat around the table with Orv,
Ruby and their two daughters, Juliet (12) and Jill (6).
When I anxiously inquired as to what we should expect of the day, Jim and I were told, "Since you arrived
ahead of schedule, why don't you two fellows help
build your classrooms and your apartments?" Garry
and Lois had their hands full moving into their house,
cleaning and making it livable after it had sat vacant
for the summer months.

"What exactly do you want us to do?" I inquired of
Orv.

"Just help out wherever you can," was his vague reply.

We silently wondered what that might mean. He informed us that he was acting as the general contractor for the construction of both teachers' apartments and the overall school facility.

The American School had been using classrooms in a facility leased from the American Baptists, located down the street from where we were eating breakfast. TASOK had outgrown this facility, so the school board, through the U.S. Embassy, had purchased property about three miles distance on a main highway leading out of town, up a hill and across from a large army base that also contained Congo President Mobutu's residence.

The property was a large triangle of mostly jungle-like land – big trees, thick bushes and dense vegetation – so there was considerable work needed to clear space for the buildings and school athletic fields. Several of the cinder-block-construction classrooms and fourplex apartments had been started, but Orv indicated that a lot of manual labor was still needed to clear brush and to dig foundation trenches.

Mid-July in the Democratic Republic of Congo is the height of the "Dry Season." Evening lows dip to the 60s and with overcast mornings, daytime highs rise only to the low 80s. Congolese consider this to be cool weather. Mid- September through mid-May marks the "Rainy Season" in that part of the world. The lows creep up to the 70s and the highs climb well into the 90s, with humidity bouncing up into the mid 80% range. Orv was dressed in a tee shirt, white shorts and tennis shoes. This attire, we discovered, was common for "European" – white, non-African – men. The pith helmet was an icon that had disappeared with Congo's independence six years earlier, but white shorts were a holdover from colonial days of the former Belgian Congo. I determined I needed to replace my bold American plaid shorts ASAP with the more appropriate white ones worn by veteran European residents.

In the short drive from the teachers' compound to the new school site, we passed the "Stanley Monument" on the right at the base of the hill. This was a large statue of British explorer Henry Morton Stanley, who in the late 1800s led a disastrous 7,000-mile African expedition to locate explorer and missionary David Livingstone. Stanley later claimed the Congo for his employer, Belgian King Leopold II, who exploited the huge area as his own private reserve known as the "Congo Free State," prior to it becoming the Belgian Congo in 1908. Congo received its independence in 1960.

At the top of the hill the main road curved and a side road split off to the left of the highway leading to the TASOK property. There were tall trees and thick vegetation on both sides of the dirt road. A six-foot chain link fence contained the school and apartment construction area. The main gate was located several hundred yards down the road in the middle of the mostly undeveloped property.

John works at apartment construction

We exited Orv's car and he introduced us to his number-one assistant and dump truck driver, David, a tall, handsome Congolese man with a flashing white-toothed smile. We were also introduced to Ron Weeks, an American missionary youth who had grown up in the Congo, and who spoke fluent Lingala, the principal African dialect of the Kinshasa area. We discovered that few of the laborers spoke any French, the official language of business and commerce. Ron had been hired by Orv to work alongside the Congolese construction supervisors and to help translate where needed. Orv spoke fluent French and also, Kituba, a second, less popular trade language known by most of the workers.

Ron was a wiry, hard working young man, responsible beyond his sixteen years. He was entering his junior year at TASOK. Ron initially served as our link to the construction site, since Jim's and my language skills were limited to English. Orv unceremoniously dumped us off and without explanation or directions, left with his assistant, David, to pick up materials and run other errands off-site.

The Congolese construction workers, scores of them, were dressed in the most amazing array of tattered rags. Some wore strings of cloth that probably used to be shirts; all had cut-offs or torn pants and most were either barefoot or had rubber flip-flops on their feet. They were short in stature, typically under 5' 6" and very skinny; zero body fat here! Some workers wore "hats" torn from the corner of cement bags; others had cloths tied around their heads. Their dark brown skin was dusty and shiny with sweat from their labors.

At the end of each workday a most amazing transformation took place, however. The workers lined up to take an outdoor bath from the few available faucets, and once cleaned up they dressed in almost identical street attire: shoes, dark slacks and long-sleeved white shirts.

They looked virtually identical to the many clerks or business people one might encounter in the city – the intent of this practice, we were told – rather than construction workers. The contrast between their work and commuter costumes couldn't have been more dramatic.

At first Jim and I thought the Congolese workers moved pretty slowly in performing their duties. We mentioned this observation on the very first noon we were transported back to the Wiebe's place for a big meal and the routine mid-day siesta of an hour or so. Both of our hosts smiled, knowingly.

Orv quietly volunteered, "Wait until you try working for a few days, all day lifting rocks and clearing brush before you come to any firm conclusions. And, try doing it with only a half a hunk of bread and some tea to fuel your efforts. Furthermore, consider that most of the workers have to get up before dawn to commute by crowded bus more than an hour to work."

After only a few days into our work routine Jim and I were frankly amazed at how much the diminutive Congolese workers actually accomplished in a day, as we fell exhausted into bed at night. How could they do this on such a meager fuel supply?

Ron proved to be an excellent cultural guide for Jim and me. We learned not to toss keys, tools or other things to the workers: "You throw things to dogs; *hand* things to people"; we learned how to use a machete to chop down brush; we learned to watch out for snakes – there were poisonous vipers in the brush; and we even learned a few words of Lingala: *Mbote* = hello; *Malamu* = good; *Malamu te* = bad; *Mabanga* = rocks; *Noke* = faster; *Malembe* = slowly; *Keba* = careful; *Tikala Malamu* = goodbye.

We also learned that we could not keep up the work pace of our young friend, Ron. I managed to sweat-soak two tee shirts a day during our construction efforts. "And this is the cool, dry season of the year? What's going to happen when it gets hot?" I wondered.

We had a lot of discoveries to make. One of those was how to navigate in our new environment.

Ron & John clear jungle at new school site

13

Sink or Swim in Kinshasa

"Not until we are lost do we begin to understand ourselves."
– Henry David Thoreau

I 've never been a particular advocate of the "sink or swim philosophy." It's always seemed a bit foolhardy or even cruel to be thrust into the deep end and expected to swim with no practice. Sometimes, however, we don't have a choice. In these instances, the experience of being in a situation that is clearly beyond one's depth can bring about a singular clarity of focus and effort. Instinct takes over from fear, powered by a strong desire for survival. Successful arrival at safety then prompts new feelings of confidence and teaches one valuable lessons in coping with unknown challenges. At least, that's been my experience.

My first swimming lesson came early on in the Congo. One morning, during our first week in Africa, Orv asked if I'd care to join him in running an errand downtown. "What a great chance to see more of Kinshasa," I thought, so I eagerly agreed. Little did I realize at the time just how exciting a routine task could be in this alien setting.

We headed off in one of the school vehicles, a tiny two door Fiat 600, to the local auto dealer to purchase a new battery for the car.

I enjoyed the 20 minute drive through the main streets of Kinshasa, circling several large round points at intersections and driving past tall buildings fifteen or more stories high that Orv indicated were where many Belgian and other Europeans resided. Even at that time of the day it smelled like *"frites"*– French fries – as we drove by. I paid little attention to the route we took since Orv confidently zipped in and out of traffic and headed directly for our destination in the business district of downtown Kinshasa.

At the Fiat dealership, Orv negotiated his business, paid for the battery and then informed me that he was going to head off to do some other business at several places in town. He indicated that his plan was to return home via taxi.

"What am I supposed to do?" I wondered.

"As soon as the workers finish installing the battery in the Fiat, just drive it back to my house taking the same route we used to get here," he directed in a matter-of-fact tone.

"Wait, wait…" I stammered, as Orv started off. "I don't think I can find my way back."

"Oh, no problem!" he exclaimed and proceeded to quickly inform me which round point to turn at before rushing off on his errands.

Inform me? I hadn't paid *any* attention to directions on the drive downtown. I had no clue in advance that he was going to ask me to drive back home. I stood there, mouth open, hesitant to call my boss back once more, fearful that I would appear as lost and helpless as I felt.

The Congolese workers at the dealership amusedly pointed my direction as I folded my 6'5" frame into the little Fiat. Taking a deep breath, I got into the car, started it up and slowly drove away from the dealership. I headed off into the dense traffic on the main boulevards of Kinshasa.

I have probably blocked out the terror I felt driving alone for the first time, knowing full well that I could not communicate with *anyone* should I have to stop for any reason on my return journey.

At the round point that appeared to best match Orv's description, I turned off taking the first street to the right. Each round point had streets heading off like spokes from a wheel, and I didn't know which spoke to follow. I made a selection and proceeded down a street. It didn't look at all familiar.

Shortly, I found myself heading into a residential area with huge walled mansions and big shade trees lining the road. The broad avenue ran along the Congo River and it was a beautiful, high-class neighborhood.

I was nearly beside myself with anxiety by that time, creeping along slower and slower as I tried unsuccessfully to figure out what I should do.

Finally, I came to a straight stretch of the shaded, tree-lined boulevard. A little guardhouse occupied the middle of the street and a striped bar blocked the road. As I approached, a helmeted, uniformed guard stepped out of the guardhouse with his rifle in one hand and held up his other, signaling for me to stop.

With a plethora of fresh "scare-the-new-arrivals" stories still echoing in my head from dinner conversations the night before, I panicked. Jamming the tiny Fiat into low gear, I floored the accelerator and spun the wheel. The car squealed on two tires right in front of the startled guard and I headed in the opposite direction. I ducked as low as I could, driving blind, head below the steering wheel in case the uniformed fellow started shooting.

The car tore away as simultaneously, the guard began to blow loud, long blasts on a whistle he had around his neck. I was sure I would be either shot or thrown in jail for life for entering some sort of "forbidden zone."

Neither happened.

After returning to the round point on the main boulevard and spending nearly an hour of driving back and forth on several other "spokes" I finally found one that led me back to the TASOK teachers' compound. I was both shaken and angry when I arrived, engine smoking, to spill out my "near death" escape to my amused hosts and fellow teachers at lunch.

When finally Orv arrived by taxi, he gave me no sympathy at all. "Hey, that's how you learn around here, by *doing*," he offered with a wry smile.

Wiebe family: Ruby, Orv, Juliet & Jill (front)

In retrospect, this first experience with being in over my head sharpened my attention to my new surroundings. I did not get lost in the city again. My driving escapade was an illustration of what students of culture call a "destabilizing" experience. These kinds of incidents hold the potential for significant personal growth. I don't think I would have been impressed with that observation at the time. I now see that it served as a valuable first lesson in facing unfamiliar and even threatening circumstances with courage and patience. I would have ample opportunity to apply this lesson repeatedly during my sojourn in the Congo.

Postscript: The guardhouse, as it turned out, marked the entry to a row of mansions occupied by Congo government officials, so access was restricted. It seems it was *not* a capital offense to turn away, after all.

14

Anticipation

*"A man begins cutting his wisdom teeth the first time he
bites off more than he can chew."*
– Herb Caen

I n spite of my wishing it away, both in restless dreams
at night and in worried thoughts during my waking
hours, the dreaded first day of classes crept ever closer.
Part of me was excited to take on the challenge of being
a teacher.

"Hmm, 'teacher.' Now *that* has a nice ring to it," I
thought.

The greater part of me, however, was simply filled
with dread: "How am I *ever* going to pull this off? What
if my students figure out I don't know what I'm doing?
What if I look like a complete *idiot* to the other teachers?
Could they send me home if I screw up too badly?"

These anxious themes echoed through my brain
with increasing frequency as I put on a confident face,

welcoming the wave of new and returning teachers who arrived in Kinshasa from their summer travels outside of the country.

The past month of our brief sojourn in the Congo had been occupied with lots of physical activity, as Jim and I daily made the trek up the hill to the new school construction site to assist in the labors there. If the truth were fully known, those short weeks had also been saturated with culture shock, huge adjustments and survival-flavored learning. In many ways it felt like we had landed on an alien planet. We had left our comfort zones far behind us and had metaphorically jumped off the bridge without first testing the bungee cord. Would we bounce back or merely splatter?

As more of the TASOK teachers arrived and the row of houses in the teachers' compound filled, Jim and I were relocated into a bedroom in the Wiebe's house, temporarily vacated by one of their daughters. The construction of our apartments on the new school site was still a couple of months away from completion.

My first year teaching assignment had been further clarified. I was assigned to teach seventh and ninth grade science courses, two sections of sophomore biology – there were a larger than expected influx of tenth graders that fall – and two sections of high school boy's P. E. I was also expected to coach TASOK's sports teams, including soccer, basketball and track.

Mr. John Franz
Eugene, Oregon
8th, 9th Science,
Biology, P.E.

"Mr. Franz" TASOK science teacher

New textbooks had arrived for the high school biology class, along with some lab materials and there were reasonably new books for the seventh grade earth science class. My principal, Orv, described the texts for the ninth grade general science class as "Pretty pathetic. Sorry. You'll have to make do somehow."

What did "make do" mean to a novice teacher like me? In 1966 the TASOK secondary school had no formal curriculum to follow, and pitifully few materials left from previous years. There was almost nothing to build from, to "make do" with, except my imagination and creativity. As if African culture shock weren't enough!

I can still picture myself sitting at a little desk in our hosts' bedroom staring at an open biology text. It was Sunday night before the Monday morning's start of school. I read and re-read Chapter One, then just stared at the pages with glazed eyes, as if somehow – magically – a plan would emerge and I would be saved from sure disaster.

My silent panicky thoughts: "What am I going to do? How did I get myself into this? There's no escape now."

I felt about as low as I can remember *ever* feeling up to that point in my young life.

Coming to my rescue, roommate Jim reassured me that the first few days of class were just *get-acquainted times*. He suggested that I think of some kind of introduction exercise since there were always new students at TASOK. He further proposed that I say a few general things about the subject of the class, even if I couldn't be more specific. That helped.

By breakfast the next morning I had *day one* figured out.

Carpe Diem!

15

A Responsive Beginning

"The crisis of today is the joke of tomorrow."
– H. G. Wells

E arth science class at the start of the next day was a breeze. The quiet, wide-eyed seventh graders seemed to hover on my every word. I promised science demonstrations and to assign science "projects" during the course of the semester. "Ooh," was the cheery, chorused response. The students' eager and supportive reactions actually prompted increased animation on my part as we went through introductions and I answered their questions.

At the bell, the beaming seventh grade students whisked out the door seemingly delighted that they had survived their first middle school experience. "I'm going to like this class!" I overheard one enthusiastic fellow tell a classmate. Little did they know their teacher shared their delight – times *two*.

Relief. A successful start.

My 10th grade biology class met the next hour. It was a different story entirely. The school was on double shifts, with slightly shorter class sessions, in anticipation of the new facility being completed in a few weeks. By *day one*, the administration had not worked out the scheduling of my two sections of Biology, so the entire group of forty-five sophomore students was crowded into a classroom that had only 30 chairs and desks. Students shared chairs, sat on desks and stood at the sides of the classroom. They packed the space. The mob of young teens was noisy, animated in reuniting with old friends and meeting new people – just plain *hyper,* might be a better descriptor. I was feeling both amused and silently apprehensive. It was hard not to be captivated by their energy. Could I channel it somehow?

After an initial greeting, some explanatory comments about dividing the class into two sections, to be accomplished the next week, and a quick round of introductions, I attempted to teach a lesson from Chapter One: "Characteristics of Living Things."

Part of my pre-breakfast brainstorm had been to capture the students' attention in this first class session with the use of a live demonstration. So, I caught a large toad that I found hopping in the yard that morning, placed it in a coffee can and brought it to class.

When I first dumped the hapless amphibian on my desk, a delighted murmur filled the room and students stood or moved so they could get a good view of my "living thing" example. I asked the class to identify the qualities of living things and then wrote their voiced comments on the blackboard. I was looking for the answer *"responsiveness"* and after no one volunteered that particular term, I picked up a yardstick that was near the desk and poked the placid toad in the rear.

Sure enough, the toad was responsive – it *hopped.* That wasn't the toad's final statement, however. His responsiveness exceeded my expectations as he then delivered a big, black *pile of feces* right on top of my desk!

A brief instant of stunned silence followed. Then, the classroom *burst* into laughter -- hoots and hysterics took over for a full five minutes. It was quite a din for the first day of class. Determining that I'd better find a way to salvage this situation and regain some semblance of control, I smiled, picked up the yardstick and scraped it across my desk with the intent of flicking the black pile out the open window adjacent to my desk.

Flick the poop, I did. However, instead of feces flying through the open, barred window, the dark blob smacked against the whitewashed wall next to the window and slowly dribbled down.

If the class' first reaction was a burst of laughter and noise, the second was an *explosion!* To cap the experience, at that *very instant* into the doorway of the classroom stepped my principal, Orv Wiebe, no doubt checking on the source of the racket. He took two paces into the room and then promptly turned on his heel and walked out. I slumped down at my desk, head on my arms and closed my eyes.

It was funny – I couldn't help laughing – but an unbelievable first day disaster.

After a few more moments of loud, lingering levity the bell rang, mercifully, and my wound up students noisily exited the room.

"Read Chapter One!" I called after them.

I don't think anyone heard me.

Postscript: I rushed to Orv's office immediately after class, imagining that he was already in the process of making arrangements to send me home. He just listened quietly to my explanation. A wry smile slowly spread across his face. "You sure know how to get their attention," he said after a poignant pause. "Try to keep the noise level down in the future." That was all he had to say about the experience.

I can't claim I did a very good job of heeding his advice.

16
Tapping Student Experience

"While we teach, we learn."
– Seneca

When you're 22 years old it is important to come across as a competent adult. Maybe especially so, since one's status in the adult world is unsettled, not fully confirmed. Facing a room full of young teenagers for the first time with zero teaching experience was therefore anxiety provoking. This challenge was compounded by a lack of resources to draw upon. These factors all came together most dramatically in my last class of that first day of teaching. It was clear from the beginning that this particular class was going to tax my courage and creativity to the limits as a fledgling teacher.

Fourteen-year-olds are interesting creatures. At the bottom of the high school status totem pole, they are especially sensitive to their peers. Desperate to fit in, they loathe being labeled odd or nerdy and crave attention. Growth spurts and hormone surges generate a kind of synergy and sparkle that can either energize a classroom or create a teacher's worst nightmare. It all depends on the quality of connection between them.

Ninth grade science concluded the glorious first day of my teaching assignment. Somewhat shaken by the biology toad experience and holding the above facts in mind, I guardedly greeted my 34 freshmen students. Since I did not wish to expose my greatest area of weakness on the first day of class, I was determined to avoid launching into *anything* academic at all costs.

The course texts were distributed and as the students thumbed through the thin, dated, simplistic material, several audible groans were voiced in the room. To me the science books seemed altogether too much like "Dick and Jane" readers. I pointed out the obvious to the class: "There is probably only enough content in your text for about a week's worth of reading…for the *whole year*. I'm told TASOK will not be able to order new books this school year. Therefore, we will be doing a lot of learning activities and independent projects in this class."

I sounded confident. Just what would those activities and projects be? I had absolutely *no clue* at that point. In truth, I was actually relieved that the students seemed far more interested in whispering to one another, checking out the opposite sex and showing off, than in probing their instructor for his class plans. The class registered no alarm at my pronouncements. I'm not altogether sure they were listening.

We proceeded with introductions. I asked each student to share where they had lived and to identify one observation in their international living or travel that they thought was interesting or weird.

Remarkably, the class entered into this exercise enthusiastically. Two of the students, brothers David and Duane Schaad, had just arrived from Angola and could only speak limited English. Later in the year they would prove to be my great allies as they were virtual prodigies in soccer, a sport I was designated to coach at the high school. I knew even less about that sport than they did about either science or English, so we struck a pragmatic and successful bargain to help one another out and to cover our respective ignorance. It worked well.

I discovered some very illuminating things in that first round of introductions. Nearly all of the students in my class had traveled and/or lived in more places on the globe than I even knew existed. As the year unfolded, whenever I started to make a reference to scientific findings from some specific location in the world, I learned to first ask if anyone in the class had either visited or lived there. By performing this ritual, I thereby saved myself the embarrassment of an inevitable public correction by one of my 14-year-old charges: "Mr. Franz, we lived there for three years and it's not like that *at all.*"

Part of teaching success comes from knowing one's audience.

While a bit intimidating, it was also plainly fascinating and impressive to see the matter-of-fact manner in which these young people traveled, adapted to change, moved through new cultures and negotiated different languages and practices. It dawned on me how much of my knowledge – even my sense of myself – was culturally dependent. I realized I had a lot to learn about living life outside of Oregon.

So, getting my ninth graders to tell their personal stories proved to be a great way to absorb a forty-five minute class period. It also seemed like a good way to connect with them personally. I wondered what I could come up with to fill *day two*. Teaching was clearly going to be a one-day-at-a-time experience.

As the ninth graders exited with the bell, I picked up my papers and headed for home. *Day one* was done. I had survived.

There *is* a God!

17

Teaching and Learning

"The greatest glory in living lies not in never falling but in rising every time we fall"
– Nelson Mandela

I didn't sink after all. In my "sink-or-swim" metaphor, after a few days of near floundering, I discovered that I could actually float, maybe even "dog-paddle" a bit. The toad-pile-stained wall was cleaned and became just a humorous memory of the first day. I came up with ideas for how and what to teach in my classes. Most of my students turned out to be remarkably able learners. They laughed at my jokes. They turned in assignments. They actually seemed interested in the subject matter I presented.

On second thought, perhaps I should qualify that last statement. *Most* of my students were willing to follow my lead, however unconventional, in the classroom. The 9th graders, however, were a different story. I'm pretty sure that age must initiate a significant hormone rush since the fourteen-year-olds in my class seemed far more interested in talking, passing notes and getting laughs from the opposite sex than paying much attention to whatever I was saying or doing in the front of the room. When combined with the "pathetic make-do" text as my only content resource, this group tapped my creativity and patience more than any other.

I decided early on to experiment with non-conventional methods of discipline since keeping some kind of order in the ninth grade classroom emerged as the first and foremost task of teaching. When students – usually the guys – disrupted class with some sort of blatant attention-grabbing antic such as tipping over backwards in their chairs or pushing a stack of books off of a desk, instead of getting angry, I determined I would adopt an "amused" posture. Perhaps I could give them what they wanted – attention – but do so in a mildly aversive manner that would discourage repeats of the disruption. Such was my reasoning, anyhow.

In response to an infraction, my retorts went something like this: "As entertaining as Tom's great fall might be, unfortunately for *Tom*, there is a natural consequence to this kind of disruption. I'm going to continue with our lesson and Tom is going to see if he can make it for five minutes with his forehead on the blackboard, feet a meter from the wall and his hands clasped behind his back. Yes, he can do this in the front of the classroom if he wishes."

P
U
N
I
S
H
M
E
N
T

F
R
A
N
Z

'S
T
Y
L
E

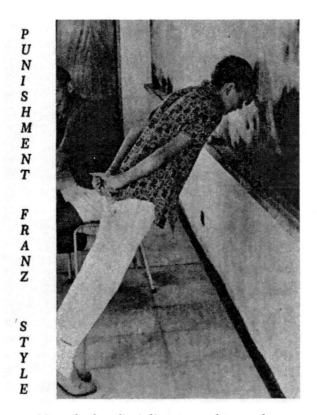

Unorthodox discipline seemed to work

I used different variations of consequences such as having the offender sit on a chair on top of a desk; having him/her stand in one place, arms straight out with one foot behind the other; asking chronic talkers to silently stand back to back and anything else I could come up with on the spot. Students appeared amused at these behavioral interventions and remarkably often they even *worked* at toning down acting-out behavior. And, sometimes they didn't.

The very first exam, prepared for my biology classes, demonstrated how my lack of teacher preparation impacted the classroom. It also illustrated the kind of steep learning curve I was on in my new role. I believe at the time I considered that first exam to be a "test of the teacher's competence" and I was determined *not* to fail in the eyes of my young charges.

It was a multiple-choice test. I assembled it over several days, writing and re-writing each question. I hoped it wouldn't be too easy. It was one of those exams where instead of providing the students with four straight-forward options, it had *five*, the last three being all or none-of-the-above or a combination of 'a' and 'b.'

Not *one* of the students in either section of my biology classes completed *all* of the test questions by the end of the hour. The students exited the classroom uncharacteristically quickly, somber and silent – almost as if in shock.

At the end of that school day, anxious for feedback, I approached a group of sophomores who were waiting at the front of the school for their ride home. "So how do you girls think you did on the test?" I asked. *"Terrible!"* was the chorus that greeted me. One shattered survivor, Ruthie, had tears running down her cheeks, "It was just *too hard*, Mr. Franz," she blurted out. "This is only the first one," I offered in a feeble attempt at encouragement. "You'll have more chances to do better."

That initial reaction sampling was a mere hint of

bad news to come. When I actually graded the exams that evening I realized even further just how far off I was in my estimation of sophomore-level test construction. The *highest score* on that first exam was *38%* and the student who achieved that elevated score was a young lady whom I was told, became a National Merit Scholar two years later. It was I who was most humbled by that experience, not my students.

Postscript: I had some red-faced apologizing to do when I next met my students face-to-face. It took several tries before I finally discovered how to make challenging but reasonable tests in my classes.

Oh, and Ruthie passed the course.

18
A Pithy Lab Experience

"Surmounting difficulty is the crucible that forms character."

– Tony Robbins

A major challenge of teaching in an African set-ting was dealing with limited resources. We were forced to make use of what we had on hand. Equipment was in chronic short supply. TASOK's sci-ence department had a few microscopes but in a Third World environment, such as ours they had a way of "walking off" sometimes even when seemingly well secured behind locked doors of a cabinet. In the night, enterprising equipment liberators removed hinges or unscrewed panels and made off with the goods, there-by providing a novice teacher like me with yet more opportunities to re-group students and revise assign-ments and expectations.

What we *did have* in abundant supply was *flora* – we

were virtually in the middle of a jungle – and *fauna* in the form of lots of toads available for dissecting. Our weekly biology lab day was thus comprised of either field trips into the jungle immediately behind the classroom, or a dissection of toads.

The most unsavory part of toad dissection was "pithing" them. This procedure involves holding the toad's head with one hand and inserting a probe quickly at the base of the cranial vault, then moving it back and forth to sever the brain and spinal cord and destroy the brain so the toad cannot feel anything. The toad is then placed "spread eagle" on a dissection pan and pins are placed in the hands and feet to hold it steady so dissection can proceed.

There were several serious challenges to this procedure when introduced by a novice biology teacher to sophomore level students. First, unlike their amphibious frog cousins, Congo toads exuded a sticky substance on the side of their heads to repel enemies. *Ewww!* Second, I discovered 15-year-olds to be a particularly squeamish lot, especially the female gender. Many had strong emotional, if not philosophical objections to performing the life-ending procedure described above. *Akkkk!* Third, *few* of my young biologists possessed the fine motor skills to get it right the first time. *Oh-Oh!*

Perhaps a specific case would best illustrate the challenges of the weekly lab sessions. One of my students, Helene, daughter of an Italian diplomat family, approached me when I first announced the notion of lab sessions in class.

"Mr. Franz, I cannot do this thing," she exclaimed. I reassured her that most people feel a bit repulsed at first, but that she'd get used to it.

"No. I *never* get used to such a horrible thing!" she insisted in her Italian English accent.

The first couple of lab sessions were predictably chaotic for more of the class than just Helene, but she clearly struggled. She sat down with her head lowered to keep from fainting. Her lab partner quietly confided to me as I passed by their station, "I don't think Helene is faking it!" I finally conceded to Helene that I would excuse her from actually performing dissections but she *would* need to participate in the lab sessions with a partner, observing and identifying the required toad systems that were being studied. She reluctantly agreed.

During the next lab session, Helene bravely stood by while her partner pithed, pinned and began slicing open the front of a toad. At the very moment Helene was leaning over the dissection pan to observe, the toad, unsuccessfully pithed, dislodged the pins in its front legs and *sat up*! Its guts spilled out the open stomach cavity.

Helene let out a blood-curdling *scream* that probably carried all the way to her native Italy. Hands in the air, she rushed out of the classroom, continuing her hysterical emanations as she ran between classrooms and out to the street in front of the school.

Realizing that I had a full-blown crisis in the making, I chased after her.

In spite of my best efforts at charm and offers of support, Helene would simply *not* be persuaded to return to the classroom that day. Somehow, she mustered the necessary courage to return the following day and in spite of a tendency to absences from recurrent bouts of "toad flu" on lab days, she eventually made it through high school biology.

Post script: After Helene's experience, I respected student resistance to a significantly greater degree. I was far less dismissive of their fears and repulsions and less rigid in my demands. I also learned the wisdom of making alternative plans in the face of compelling resistance.

Sophomore biology never lacked enthusiasm

19

Leisure Life in the Congo

"In our leisure we reveal the kind of people we are."
– Ovid

A long with the challenges of adapting to a new role as teacher, came the issue of managing time *outside* of the classroom. This was no minor concern for an active, adventuresome young adult such as I, recently unplugged from what might be safely characterized as a robust social environment. Dating, movies, parties, friends, television, restaurants, athletic events and other regular leisure diversions had suddenly vanished, were unfamiliar or simply inaccessible in this new setting. I was faced with re-inventing this important part of my life.

In anticipating a two-year assignment in Africa, I somehow fantasized that the absence of familiar social diversions would prompt me to evolve into some sort of a contemplative stoic. With this notion in mind, I packed and shipped an entire trunk full of college novels and text books that I hadn't taken time to read during my university sojourn, but that I pictured myself pouring over during my stay in the Congo.

22-year-olds are capable of generating a rich fantasy life, all right.

Of course, at the end of two years in the tropics, the only attention those volumes received was from mold spores. *They* poured over the books, all right! At one point I even signed up for a correspondence course from the University of Nebraska intending to pick up some needed credits. I later dropped out because I was simply too busy and distracted to complete the tedious reading/writing requirements.

I reluctantly have to conclude that we "take us with us" no matter how far across the world we might venture.

I also had my father's advice to reflect on as I anticipated leisure time use prior to my arrival in Africa. In our drive to the Portland train station departure, Dad attempted to shore up my moral fiber with a pointed fatherly warning: "You know, John, you have had an active dating life during college. There will surely be sexual temptations for nice-looking young men like you when you're far from home. *Don't give in to them!*"

I was tempted to point out to Dad that I had *actually* already had practice in the sexual temptation-resistance business, but this did not seem like a good topic for light conversation at the time. It invited further probing that would not be productive, at least not from my point of view.

I remembered as a seven-year-old, innocently inquiring how babies came about at the dinner table one evening. Mom and Dad exchanged glances. Then, on cue, Dad had taken me from the dinner table, where my 11-year-old sister was cracking up with laughter, to my bedroom for a private father-son talk about sex.

Dad's sex instruction began and ended with references to farm animals copulating, none of which I had ever witnessed or could even imagine. "What did *that* have to do with my question," I wondered? Dad was the only one in the room who had grown up on a farm. I don't think I had ever even *visited* a farm. Finally, in exasperation, Dad concluded "You need to ask your mother about this!" and with that, he left the room.

Regarding Dad's advice to me on remaining celibate in Africa? I just thanked him for his concern, and said, "OK, I'll watch out."

Oh, I *did* ask Mom about the babies, by the way.

So what actually occupied our leisure time in Kinshasa? There were two or three movie theatres in town but we seldom went there; they showed only French language films. Sometimes, however, an older movie we had already seen in the U.S. was featured.

Jim and I then attended for a diversion since we already knew the plot, even if we couldn't understand the French-dubbed words. The U.S. Information Service periodically received first-run English-language films from the States and if we were able to maneuver an invitation from someone in the diplomatic community we eagerly attended these events.

Restaurants in Kinshasa were typically quite expensive and difficult to navigate without an interpreter. Our first restaurant outing with some other young American volunteers illustrated this point. Two of our party ordered, "filet Americain" from the menu imagining it to be a safe choice. It sounded familiar, anyhow. What arrived at the table was a mound of uncooked ground beef with a raw egg in the center.

"What lousy food preparation," we reasoned.

Great confusion ensued as our dinner partners tried to persuade a puzzled Congolese server to return their entrée to be cooked.

We were later informed that the entrée *had* been properly prepared.

It was mostly *people* that filled our free time. TASOK followed a weekday schedule that took an extended two-hour mid-day break. While some people used the time to eat lunch and take a siesta, most of us single teachers and many of the older high school students and other American volunteers in Kinshasa went swimming two or three times a week at the local Lycée Royale (European secondary school) that had an Olympic sized pool. This was a great place to socialize. As the year progressed, I found myself looking forward to informal visits with Betty Jean Rempel when we went swimming.

Jim and I received numerous invitations to dine with other TASOK teachers and with many of the Kinshasa-based missionary families. Sometimes after dinner we played table games, but more often it was just a time of conversation and sharing stories. These were welcome diversions and surprisingly positive experiences. Up to that point in time I had never imagined that it could be entertaining to simply spend an evening interacting with others. My previous definition of a fulfilling night out would have been attending a movie or ball game, or dining at a restaurant, not story-telling at someone's residence.

Two specific impressions stood out from those evenings spent with career missionaries in the Congo. Unfortunately, neither was particularly positive. First, it was surprising to me that few of the people we dined with appeared to have meaningful personal relationships with Congolese. While many of the missionaries worked alongside nationals during daylight hours, they worshipped and socialized separately. Rarely did we witness any Kinshasa-based missionaries socializing with Africans other than on structured occasions such as a school graduation or celebration of some kind.

The stories we heard from those who lived and worked in rural settings ("the bush") painted a different picture, however. We were told that expatriates and nationals alike shared personal concerns and prayer with one another and regularly enjoyed common worship and social interaction. Perhaps it was the presence of an English-language church and more social opportunities with peers in the city that made the difference.

A second impression was even more troubling to me, however. On several occasions we dined with long-term missionaries who were consistently and bluntly negative in their appraisal of Congolese.

"The help can't be trusted; you have to check on them constantly."

"Given half a chance, they'll steal you blind."

"If you want something done right, you have to do it yourself. Congolese have no appreciation for quality."

"Everyone in this country has got an angle or a con. We have to keep our guard up, constantly."

These kinds of comments were pretty disturbing to us idealistic 20-something-year-olds. At best, they seemed inconsistent with an appreciation of African people and at worst they came across as crass racist generalizations.

Jim and I puzzled over this privately to one another. On one particular occasion I impulsively asked a dinner host, "If it's *that* bad and you feel *that* strongly, what keeps you here in the Congo?"

That was a conversation stopper.

After an awkward pause, the reply I received was something like, "We're here to serve the Lord. These frustrations represent trials and testing that are part of ministry in Africa."

The negative comments we heard, stated in English, were frequently shared within the earshot of Congolese kitchen workers. House workers were always addressed in Lingala or Kituba, the local languages. Most spoke a little French, but none spoke English to our knowledge. Some house help had served the same families for fifteen or twenty years. We wondered how many of these veterans secretly understood the pejorative comments being made so openly by their missionary employers.

In 1966 there was a significant contingent of young people performing volunteer service in Kinshasa and elsewhere in the Congo with the Mennonite Central Committee. MCC was the same faith-based social service organization Dad worked with during World War II. Their generic service program was called PAX (for "peace"), and the 19 to 21-year-old male volunteers were known as "PAX-men." They humorously referenced their female counterparts as "TamPAX," but never to their face. We played volleyball, went on picnics and shared outings to local swimming sites or beaches outside the city with these young adults. They formed the core of our social network.

The camaraderie of peers in a foreign environment was a good thing. Sometimes the combination of boredom, youthful risk-taking and naiveté got away from us, however.

Jim & John at the Stanley Monument, Congo River

20

Congo Police Stop

"The way out of trouble is never as simple as the way in."
– Edgar Watson Howe

One day Jim and I accompanied three PAX-men friends on an excursion into downtown Kinshasa. I can't remember the original purpose of the trip, but it seems likely we were headed for "Wimpy's," a popular restaurant near the city center that we had discovered served American-style hamburgers and milkshakes.

As we entered the intersection of a round point near the downtown area, a Congolese policeman directing traffic from a pedestal in the middle of the intersection, turned. He held his arms out for our lane of traffic to stop. Our vehicle had already entered the intersection, so we continued on through. A VW Kombi full of white men crossing against the stop signal triggered an immediate response. The policeman began rapidly blowing on his whistle for us to stop. The PAX-men yelled to our driver in unison, *"Go!"* and he punched the accelerator.

We continued down the broad "Avenue 30 Juin" but very soon we discovered that we were being pursued. A taxi was rapidly gaining on us, lights blinking and horn honking repeatedly. A policeman, head and shoulders projecting outside a rear window, was whistling and gesturing wildly at us. It looked remarkably like an African episode of "Keystone Kops."

At that point in time, the Kinshasa police had no vehicles of their own and so they commandeered taxis to pursue traffic violators. We had already been briefed repeatedly in dinner conversations with local missionaries, that traffic stops of Europeans were typically an opportunity for underpaid local police to shake-down whites. Offering advice that likely never made it to church deputation services, we were encouraged *not to stop* if whistled down. We followed this advice.

Our young PAX-man driver gunned the VW engine and commenced a series of tire-squealing turns down side streets around the main boulevard. The Congolese taxi driver proved to be up to the challenge, however, matching our various turns and speed and eventually catching up to us. It was an exciting chase, but having never fled from police before, we didn't know what to expect once we were caught.

Unable to drop his pursuer, our young PAX-man driver pulled over as the irate Congolese policeman ran up to our vehicle. The five of us young men filed out. The officer appeared *livid*, loudly yelling and angrily, animatedly gesticulating at our vehicle and at us. None of our wide-eyed group could understand a word he said. We understood the emotions directed our way, however.

Now what would happen, we wondered?

Hearing all the commotion, a European man emerged from an office adjacent to where we were stopped. In perfect English, he told us "Please let me handle this," a request we were all too glad to grant. He then proceeded to engage the policeman in a lengthy and intense conversation in French.

As we watched, the Congo cop's affect changed. His eyes suddenly got big. He somberly glanced back and forth from us to the European merchant. Finally, the officer stiffened his posture, mustered all of his dignity, slowly and formally saluted, then turned and with head held high, sauntered off down the street. At that point, the taxi driver initiated a huge din, quieted only when our European savior placed a couple of Congo franc bills in his hand. The driver, grumbling and flashing angry backward looks, finally drove away in his taxi.

The man who rescued us introduced himself as a Dutch merchant who had reportedly perfected his English by watching the popular western *Bonanza* on TV. He let us know he had employed a little creativity on our behalf. He had reportedly informed the traffic policeman that the five of us *"Mondeles"* – white men – were very well connected with the government. If the officer persisted in making trouble for us he would be duly reported and "squished" by his superiors. Apparently the agitated cop did not want to take the chance of testing out whether or not this was true.

The Dutch gentleman also gave us a short lesson on dealing with local police. We learned that we should never directly look at a Congolese traffic cop, or we would surely be whistled down. *Europeans* virtually never made eye contact with police, but *Americans* often did, according to our amused benefactor. Hence, our higher rate of shakedown stops.

Once again, even a simple trip to town became an adventure.

Police stand at intersection – don't make eye contact!

21
Taking Things Too Far

"Once we accept our limits, we go beyond them."
– Albert Einstein

Teaching science classes at TASOK without training, resources or experience presented some unique challenges for me as a novice instructor. Throughout the two years I spent at the task it was always a scramble to come up with new ways to present content that captured students' attention and still stayed within the boundaries of the subject matter. A couple of examples might serve as an illustration of my attempt at rising to meet this challenge.

The pathetic ninth grade science text contained a chapter on *driving safety*. This was not a particularly engaging topic to my class since they were all 15 years old with zero personal experience in driving. Few of even the older students at TASOK were permitted to drive in Kinshasa since operating a vehicle in that

Third World metropolis was a remarkably dangerous undertaking. There were no operational traffic signals but only round points at main intersections, sporadically occupied by traffic policeman. Their contribution to order, as previously noted, was more often directed by politics and economics than by rule of law.

Entering any intersection in the city was essentially a life-threatening experience. We operated by the principle, "s/he who hesitates is lost." That is, one adopted a driving strategy consisting of a certain "I-own-the-road" bravado that kept one's vehicle in motion, foot poised above the brake and peripheral vision at high alert. The main boulevards were broad, three or four lanes across, but as they approached the downtown area, cars would sometimes crowd five or six across. If progress were blocked, some enterprising drivers wouldn't hesitate to use the sidewalks or other spaces to bypass traffic jams.

Kinshasa driving was a wonder to behold and a terror to navigate. Few parents or guardians were willing to subject their high school-aged students to this particular driver's training environment.

One point my ninth grade science text made about safe driving had to do with maintaining a proper distance from the vehicle in front. The higher the rate of speed, the longer the required stopping distance. Simple book, simple point. The book had a chart that identified approximate stopping distances at different speeds. For example, at 15 mph it indicated that it typically took 47 feet to stop; at 25 mph, 130 feet; and at 40 mph, 335 feet.

I thought it might be more meaningful if we actually tested the book's numbers out with an experiment. Students might be better able to visualize the distances if they had a *live demonstration*, I reasoned. Also, it simply seemed like a good way to fill a class period; far more interesting than sitting indoors for a boring lesson.

So, I lined the ninth graders up on either side of the dirt road in front of the school, drew a line across the road with a stick and drove the school's VW Kombi at the different text book speeds down the road, slamming the brakes on at the line in the dirt. The vehicle skidded to a stop in a cloud of dust and the students then employed a long tape measure I'd borrowed from the school's shop to check the distance of the skid marks. We compared our test results to the figures in the textbook.

The above description doesn't come close to capturing the excitement and drama of the actual event, however. As I neared the line on the first two runs the students cheered, whooped and hollered before being totally engulfed in a huge dust cloud. The kombi bounced and skidded, semi-fishtailing as I locked the brakes.

I was frankly a bit nervous as I prepared to drive back for the final 40 mph run. I directed the students to step back even farther from the street. When I finally slammed on the brakes at 40 mph, the vehicle skidded, careening down the dirt road for well over 100 yards, nearly tipping over at one point.

The ninth grade girls screamed and the guys yelled loud cheers, while TASOK's principal Orv, in alarm, dashed out of the main administration building toward us. Several other teachers and a small crowd of students had also emerged from their open windowed classrooms to see what all the commotion was about. Orv flung open the car door as I sat gripping the wheel, eyes closed, forehead resting on the top, heart still beating madly in my throat.

"What was *that* all about?" he demanded.

After offering explanations and apologies and promising never to repeat such foolishness again, I returned to my classroom surrounded by my still laughing and chattering ninth grade students. I know they learned *something*, but I suspect it wasn't what I had intended.

Incidentally, the skid marks of our VW Kombi on the sandy dirt road consistently exceeded the numbers in our textbook, yet another illustration of how easy it is to *take things too far!*

22

Innovation & Awkwardness

"It is the answers, not the questions, that are embarrassing."
– Helen Suzman

A nother example of my attempts to be creative with classroom activities is illustrated by a class assignment on first aid techniques. Someone, likely the parent of one of the students, had donated medical supplies, so we had available for classroom use rolls of gauze, tape and even some splints.

After instructing students on recommended procedures for burns, broken bones, poisoning, shock, transportation of victims and even pre-CPR – today's version emerged in the 70s – in class lectures and demonstrations, we had a day of practical testing.

Students were assigned to small groups for the purpose of assessing their ability to apply first aid to hypothetical victims. They were told that they would be evaluated on accuracy, authenticity and speed in applying appropriate measures. Each group was given a complicated scenario to address. One or two group members were designated to be victims that fit the scenario and the rest were to be considered first aid rescuers. The victims in the designed scenarios were afflicted with a plethora of co-occurring symptoms: e.g. they were drunk, with broken bones, burned, poisoned and in shock, etc. Each group had to assess the key issues and apply the appropriate first aid measures in proper sequence. They were then to transport their assigned victim out of the classroom to a meeting point by the edge of campus.

The above directions quickly transformed the assignment into a *competition*. Perhaps it seems obvious now, but I simply had not anticipated this outcome. At the signal to begin, the student groups quickly figured out their strategy, began winding gauze and tape on the "victims", most of whom got into their role with enthusiastic wails of pain and anguish. Staggering under the load, the teams each provided cross-handed transport of their subjects out of the classroom, down the main walkway through campus and over to the assigned destination.

What made this a memorable event were not just the dramatic splints and wrappings of the victims – some looked like mummies! – but also their loud moans and groans, accompanied by the laughter and cheers of encouragement offered by team members as they rushed to the rendezvous point. Most teams had repeated spills en route that heightened the drama and antics.

Of course, since this all took place on the TASOK campus, there were few classes that *weren't* disrupted by the racket taking place outside their open windows. Once again, principal Orv came running, and once again after explanations and apologies, academic life returned to normal at TASOK. Students seemed delighted to have the opportunity to experience a little "drama" in their instruction. Perhaps my neighbor and friend, Jim, who actually taught the subject, had unduly influenced me.

. . . .

A final example that documents my first-year-of-teaching challenge of figuring out how to present subject matter came in the form of discomfort I experienced in introducing the topic of sex and reproduction to my biology classes. As the week approached for my class to cover this popular topic, I became increasingly nervous. At age 22, the thought of standing in front of a room full of young teenagers, saying "penis" and "vagina" out loud and explaining menstruation…well, it seemed a bit overwhelming! I couldn't *skip* the topic: several students had informed me with broad smiles that they were *really* looking forward to *that chapter*! How would I pull this off?

I finally determined that I would get to school early,

draw a series of labeled diagrams on the blackboard, and then mostly point while I made my clinical explanations. I even practiced my lecture the night before, a *first* in my abbreviated teaching career.

On the morning of the sex lecture, I was already nervously pitted out before class began. Lacking time for a shirt change, I welcomed the class and launched into the day's lesson. I managed to identify the male and female sex organs and functions by name without my voice cracking, though I will admit that the terms were spoken very rapidly. No eye contact was made or attempted on my part. I quickly and succinctly described the basics of the anatomy, physiology and process of human reproduction. There was a lot to cover in 45 minutes. Somehow, I made it all the way through that lecture!

The students certainly must have picked up on their teacher's lack of comfort with the subject matter, since uncharacteristically, there was minimal chatter at the end of class. The room emptied more quickly than usual.

Except for Linda Sue.

Linda Sue was a pretty little dark-haired gal from somewhere in the Deep South of the U.S. My impression of her was that she was a bit boy-crazy, a flirt who typically had her blouse unbuttoned at least one button lower than her female classmates.

Not that I ever noticed, of course.

After the class had cleared the room, Linda Sue

sauntered up to my desk with a knowing smile on her bright young face. She drawled, "Mr. Franz, that was a fine class, but there *are* a couple of things you didn't get quite right." She proceeded to offer *her* version of details about menstruation and even made a comment or two about intercourse.

In fairness, it wasn't lewd or a veiled come-on, just informative, almost patronizing in a kindly way. I was so shocked by this update that I didn't fully register the details she shared. When Linda Sue finished setting the record straight, she parted with something like, "I hope that helps. Bye-now." She swished out of the classroom to join her friends while I sat there with my mouth open.

I guess it was pretty obvious to more than just me that I still had *a lot* to learn.

Novice science teacher figuring out what to do next

23

More Lively Lessons from Biology

"If you're going to live by the river, make friends with the crocodile."

– Indian Proverb

Moving to Africa from Oregon introduced novel encounters with more than the local populace, a whole new world of living things became part of my unfolding experience as well. From my first introduction to cockroaches, mosquitoes and wall lizards to my discovery of an unlimited supply of dissecting toads, it was evident that I was no longer in familiar environs.

Early on we learned from our dinner hosts that in that part of Africa, most big game animals had long since disappeared or had fled to less populated, more remote areas. So much for the fantasies of seeing elephants, giraffes or leopards move stealthily through the jungle foliage behind our school.

We *did* have some resident monkeys, however, at least in the first year of my two-year teaching stint. The screeching simians and a variety of tropical birds provided a very effective exotic distraction through the open, barred classroom windows whenever any of us instructors got too boring to hold the full attention of our students.

One rather unsettling set of community members that were in residence particularly at the new school site was poisonous vipers. These slow-moving, well-camouflaged, seriously dangerous snakes made their appearance mostly at night. If the ground was smooth you could actually see snake trails with a flashlight or at first light in the morning. We understood why Congolese homes always had packed dirt yards around their dwellings, typically swept clean by the residents. No lawns to mow there!

We occasionally found vipers in piles of debris or under tarps or other items left out over night. Vipers are relatively slow, at least the ones we encountered and therefore not especially a threat unless disturbed by surprise. Their presence was a *disincentive* for most Euro-Americans like us to walk about barefoot. They also prompted us to carry and use flashlights whenever moving about school property at night.

One of my biology students, Jim Miller, was the son of a medical doctor who had a strong interest in *herpetology*, the study of amphibians and reptiles such as snakes and crocodiles. Jim's dad, Dr. John Knox

Miller, a well-known Presbyterian medical missionary and co-founder of the Institut Medical Chretien
du Kasai, a medical teaching institute and hospital,
was an avid amateur snake collector. He was known
to send home to museums in the states, live rare specimens in colleagues' carry-on luggage, unannounced
to airline officials. Somehow, in today's heightened
TSA airport scrutiny, I seriously doubt this practice
would be possible.

Jim approached me at one point and inquired if I
might be interested in his obtaining some live animal
specimens from the interior where his parents served.
He indicated that his dad was always catching interesting things and Jim proposed, "As a biology teacher,
I thought you might like to show the students some
real wildlife."

After further discussion, I expressed interest in
two unique samples: a crocodile and a boa constrictor.
"Could your father capture and deliver these animals
to me?" I inquired, half in jest. Jim promised to see
what he could do the next time he went home to visit
his parents in the interior.

I honestly didn't think Jim was serious about
obtaining these unique Congo creatures, but I proceeded to negotiate with my skeptical principal Orv
for a large 50-gallon drum to be used for a crocodile,
should it somehow join us. I'm pretty sure Orv didn't
think it was likely to happen either.

A few weeks later, after I had totally forgotten

about the far-fetched discussion, Jim showed up at the classroom door one Monday morning surrounded by an excited, noisy group of classmates. He was holding a big burlap sack away from his side. It contained something heavy.

"Here's your croc!" he proudly proclaimed as I approached in total disbelief.

A peek into the sack revealed a meter-long live crocodile, just as promised. We carried the croc to the drum located behind the classroom, placed some big rocks in the bottom and partially filled it with water, before introducing "Marvin," the name students chose for the amphibian, to his new home.

Jim Miller & John with Marvin the croc

Marvin was quite a spectacle and conversation piece for weeks and months to come, especially when it came time for his feeding. Every week or so we would place some raw meat, chicken or beef, on the end of a stick and then place it near the side of Marvin's mouth. He would swing around sharply and grab the meat in one bite, sometimes taking the end of the stick with a hearty chomp.

Regularly, we had to dump out and replace the feces-contaminated water in his drum. This was also a source of student interest. Marvin came scampering out of the drum into a small fenced area we created for the task and depending on his mood, he either sunned himself quietly, or circled the fence rapidly to the screams of his young audience.

While he may have been pleased with his popularity, Marvin unfortunately, perhaps predictably, did not live a long, healthy life. By the time he expired after nearly a year with us, he had grown a foot or more in length, but I regret to admit, the toxic environment of his living conditions likely took their toll.

My TASOK students demanded a memorial ceremony upon learning of Marvin's demise. They created a headstone and with some very clever, humorous and sentimental words of dedication, we buried him on the edge of the TASOK schoolyard.

Rest in peace, Marvin.

Grieving student Dave H. at Marvin's grave

24

Dinner with Herman

"Nothing in life is to be feared. It is only to be understood."
– Marie Curie

J ust a few weeks after Marvin's arrival, our second and more successful exotic Congo native made his appearance on site. When Jim obtained Marvin the croc, he managed to transport him on a direct private Missionary Aviation Fellowship (MAF) flight from his parent's rural station to Kinshasa, with the amused but cautious cooperation of the pilot.

This time, Jim had obtained a boa constrictor to bring to his biology teacher, but he was returning to Kinshasa on an Air Congo DC-3 commercial flight. No problem. Jim placed the large, coiled serpent into a gunnysack tied at the top and with the help of another high school buddy, they lugged it onto the flight as carry-on, placed at Jim's feet.

According to the story told to me, somewhere

mid-flight a Congolese stewardess inquired about the contents of the burlap bag. Note: in 1966, Air Congo passengers typically carried on board all manner of materials and sizes of items, not trusting sticky-fingered airport handlers to deliver their checked baggage intact. Jim reportedly replied straight-faced to the stewardess that he had a huge snake in the sack. Convinced he was kidding, she did not pursue the matter further at the time. That is, until Jim was in the process of deplaning. She then asked, in jest, to see the snake. Jim complied. The bloodcurdling screams and record emptying of the plane that followed sent all the students who accompanied Jim into gales of laughter as they recited the incident to me.

I named the boa "Herman the German Worm" for no other reason than I liked the silly sound of it. The moniker produced smiles whenever he was introduced. Herman was 2 meters 43 centimeters in length – almost exactly eight feet – and heavy. My amused and helpful principal, Orv, came through once again and had his workmen build a heavy wire cage that measured two feet square and ten feet long to house Herman.

Like other constrictors, TASOK's "big squeeze" only needed to feed every month or two depending upon the size of his meal. The caveat was that he had to consume *live* food, i.e. to kill and swallow his meals. That presented a challenge. For some time, I paid Congolese workers to catch good-sized rats for Herman's meals. They had difficulty capturing them *alive*, however, and were unhappy with me each time I refused to accept the battered, expired specimens they furnished for Herman's dining pleasure. Finally, I arranged with one of the local missionaries in town to purchase small rabbits he raised and had in abundance at his home.

Biology comes alive – Herman the boa

Feeding day for Herman was an interesting spectacle, if you've never seen a boa at work before. A live little dinner (rat, rabbit) would be loosed in the cage. At first the serpent seemingly ignored this introduction.

Then, the boa would come alive and slowly stalk its prey, tongue flicking, head and eyes riveted on the live animal. Suddenly, in a lightning-fast move, the snake's mouth would grab its meal and quickly coil about it.

It was exciting enough to take your breath away! It certainly did so for the small prey. Then, when its dinner stopped wiggling, the boa would open its jaws and slowly the inert meal would disappear into its interior, a large lump marking its progress to the center of the constrictor.

I ran into trouble the first time I switched from big ugly rats to cute little bunnies. I found the feeding process fascinating, way beyond anything I had ever seen in *my* high school biology class, that's for sure. My students, however, were considerably less impressed with the whole process than I, especially the girls. Some of the fellows begged to be informed as to when the next feeding would occur, but most of the girls wanted *nothing* to do with it.

On the day prior to first introducing a new source of live food – a young rabbit – I duly informed my classes that I planned to feed Herman the following morning. Students were invited to come early to class if they'd like to witness it. A few did. Most came to class right at the bell.

The cage was in the back of my classroom. I had introduced the bunny into the cage first thing in the morning, but Herman ignored it. He lay inert. The bunny hopped all over the huge coiled snake but there was no apparent response. Classes came and went. The girls expressed dismay that a cute little bunny was in the cage with the big bad boa, but nothing was happening so class proceeded as usual.

I had a class period free during the mid-morning and it was at that point in time as I was sitting at my desk in the front of the room, grading papers, I heard a loud sound like air rushing out of a tire. Startled, I looked up just in time to see Herman in strike position. He grabbed the rabbit, quickly coiled and constricted around it and as he did so the bunny let out a long, high-pitched sound somewhere between a whistle and a falsetto-scream. It echoed across my empty cement-block-construction classroom, out the open windows and across the TASOK campus.

Most of the high school students recognized the source of the sound. Many were horrified by it. In more than one classroom, girls started crying and several concerned, angry and shocked teachers rushed into my room as the bell rang for the change of classes. The rabbit's hind feet were still sticking out of Herman's mouth by the time my colleagues made it to the back of my classroom to investigate the source of the scary noise.

Postscript: I was amused but also surprised at the strong reaction my live African specimen had produced, both among students and instructors. This was before reality television, so it's possible the same quality of reaction wouldn't be witnessed today. I also found it important to promise my tolerant and amused principal, that all future feedings would be initiated *after* regular school hours.

25

Camping in the Congo

"Let's go surfin' now, Everybody's learning how, come on a safari with me"
– *Surfin' Safari*, Beach Boys, circa 1962

I 'm not sure whose idea it was to go camping on the Congo coast during spring break. I do know that by the end of March 1967, we were very ready for a break, both students and teachers alike. In a letter I sent to my sister at the time, I noted:

> *"...the last couple of weeks were really tough ones. The kids were very restless and generally pretty unresponsive. I'm hoping everyone, myself included, will come back from spring break full of enthusiasm for biology and general science."*

Wishful thinking, indeed.

Some of the inspiration for this particular adventure

must surely go to the Beach Boys, of all people. Between their hit tunes of *"Surfin' Safari"* and *"Surfin' USA,"* released during this era, we had this ingrained idea that we should be doing something very cool like *surfing* during our time off. Twenty-something young adults are pretty locked into the culture's musical icons and we were no exception. We were headed to the Congo coast to go "surfin'!"

Note: this experience also qualified as an "adventure" since it had *some* planning associated with it, but the actual unfolding of events was pretty unpredictable. That adventures are nearly always unpredictable was certainly confirmed in our two week get-away.

There were five of us that headed out on this voyage from Kinshasa to the coast of the Congo. I was the driver of our TASOK Kombi van. My roommate and fellow teacher, Jim, was a second member of the group. A 20-year-old easy-going art student, Dave Hastings, who was volunteering with the Baptists for a year, was the third member. The remaining two were high school students.

One student, Ron Weeks, has been previously described. He was our cultural guide and fellow construction laborer during the first few weeks of our arrival in the Congo. Ron, aka "Ronnie", was a personable, low-key high school junior fluent in Lingala and very Congo-acculturated.

In contrast to his persona, the final member of our travel team was an energetic, full-of-spunk senior,

Jimmy Shafe, who was both fearless and fun, his wits and humor as sharp as a tack! We also included in our motley entourage, Ronnie's dog, whose name escapes me after 45 years. I'll call him "Rusty" for lack of a better moniker. His presence proved to be a successful deterrent to would-be thieves and military hitchhikers on our journey.

We packed up the vehicle with a lot of food, a few clothes, mostly shorts and tee shirts, and some camping gear including a tent, sleeping bags, some pots and pans.

We headed for the coast of Congo some 420 miles away. Anxious to squeeze out all the vacation time we could, we departed from Kinshasa at 11 pm on the day school was out, a Thursday. We drove through the night on the paved *National 1* highway, heading for the port city of Matadi, some 200+ miles away.

The road to Matadi was "paved" after a fashion. Several years of tropical rainstorms and heavy trucks left sections with gaping holes as if hit by small mortars. It was a real chore to avoid the large potholes in the blacktop and to dodge the periodic wrecks that were just left standing in the roadway, and still make decent time. Every so often the pavement would be completely washed out and we'd have to creep along an off-road dirt trail diversion. We were stopped at two army roadblocks along the way, but fortunately neither proved to be a problem. At one of them, we had to honk to wake up the soldiers at the barrier.

Daybreak made its abrupt appearance at 6:15 am. We had arrived at the Matadi ferry crossing at about 5:30 am, bleary-eyed and anxious as daybreak approached. What we came upon was the wildest imaginable assortment of beat-up trucks lined up for blocks and blocks waiting to get onto the space-limited ferry. The vessel itself held only two big trucks and four cars for each river crossing.

Checking out the ferry at Matadi

"Oh brother," we lamented to one another, "this is going to take all day!"

We walked several blocks down to the waterfront to check out the situation and to find some fresh bread to buy for breakfast. As we approached the ferry some soldiers approached us and demanded to see our papers, quizzing us as to our destination and reason for travel. Fortunately, Ron was both fluent and clever in his explanations and managed to get them chuckling at some comment of his. The soldiers left us alone without demanding any money or hassling us further.

A policeman at the water front barrier eventually conveyed some good news. He informed us that we could drive around the lines and take priority over the queue of commercial vehicles since we were driving a passenger car.

We patiently waited along with crowds of people gathering to pile onto the first ferry crossing of the day. At 7:30 am sharp a policeman blew his whistle and the race was on! A ten-ton truck nearly smashed into our van as I raced the kombi up the ramp and onto the ferry.

When the fortunate first six vehicles made it onto the vessel, filling its space, the officer allowed the waiting mob to board. There was another rush of urgency and excitement as people poured onto the ferry. Most were women, many of whom did an impressive job of balancing heavy loads as they climbed aboard. The Congolese mamas carried babies on their backs while at the same time they carried huge bundles on their heads.

"That's something you'll never see in Oregon," I wryly commented to Jim.

My written comment to my sister regarding this

scene noted, *"you could actually smell the people coming for nearly a quarter of a mile."* What a cacophony of unforgettable colors, sounds, and odors! That would be a sensory experience hard to duplicate, challenging to even describe.

The Matadi ferry was the only means of crossing the broad, deep, and rapid Congo River at that point in time. Later, by 1983 I have been told, a suspension bridge was built at that very location, taking a good deal of drama away from this particular experience.

Once across the Congo River, we still had another 125 miles to go to reach our destination, the small seaside community of Muanda on the coast. The road from Matadi to our destination was very different from our previous one. One lane, unpaved, often muddy with huge ruts and holes, it took us nearly eight hours to drive the stretch. Giant Mercedes diesel trucks, like the ones lined up at the ferry, used and abused this road along with smaller vehicles like ours. Many times, even employing first gear in the VW Kombi seemed too fast. Miraculously, we only got stuck once. With four able-bodied pushers we were successful in freeing ourselves with little delay.

At one point, as we came to an open stretch of road, a herd of long-horned cattle blocked the road. We honked and yelled but the animals just stood there, amusedly watching this bunch of funny-looking white guys make noise. Finally, after the four of my passengers climbed out of the vehicle and charged, waving arms in the air at the stubborn bovines, we got enough of them to step aside that I could drive through the herd. Jimmy claimed that that was the first time he had actually seen cattle in the Congo. I don't think any of us hoped we'd see any more of them.

We camped right on the beach at Muanda. Right on the beach. Our campsite was adjacent to an inlet created by a stream that emptied into the ocean. Some visitors to the area told us we could wade into the water up to our waist and feel for oysters with our feet, then reach down to harvest them. I'm not a shellfish fan so I took a pass on that experience.

We erected our 2-½-man tent. There were five of us, so obviously three fellows ended up sleeping somewhere else most nights. It was so warm and breezy at the beach that we had no problem sleeping outside. No problem, that is, until it started raining! After two successful nights in the open, our luck ran out.

It started raining on Sunday afternoon and continued to *pour* for the next two and a half days. The storm was a strong one, generating strong winds and unusually high tides that swept into our tent, soaking the bedding. The five of us had to ditch the outdoors experience and *try* to sleep under cover for two straight nights. It was pretty miserable. We did our cooking and waiting out the storm during the day from the shelter of an outdoor porch at an abandoned Belgian house near where we had camped.

What did we eat? Well, we purchased fresh bread

locally, along with fruit such as mangos, pineapple and seedy oranges. I recall that our diet was pretty lacking in anything green. We brought along some canned chili, tuna, pancake mixes and cheese. I can't remember what else we consumed. We also bought a fresh fish from a local fellow walking the beach and pan-fried it up. Since the five of us are all still alive it's safe to conclude that our menu was sufficient to sustain life.

Sleeping? We took the seats out of the van and two of our number, the high school kids, Jimmie and Ronnie, slept on the kombi's bench seats on the porch of the abandoned house. The other three of us somehow tried to stretch out, more likely, *curl up*, inside the van. The abandoned house was locked up tight, unoccupied and empty. We didn't consider breaking in.

Our camping trip was off to an exciting start. It soon became even more of an adventure.

26

Malaria and the Ladies of the Night

"I bless the rains down in Africa,
Gonna take some time to do the things we never have..."
– "Africa" Toto, 1982

I f things hadn't taken enough of a turn to the dark side with the raging storm, Sunday night I came down with malaria. I had felt tired and achy all day, but assumed that it was all the horsing around in the surf, our version of "surfing", combined with sleep deprivation.

As the night progressed, however, I started sweating profusely and then got the shakes. My head ached, as did all of my joints. I had diarrhea and had to find a bush behind which to relieve myself repeatedly in the pouring rain. Toilet paper was pretty useless in those conditions. I felt miserable!

At some point a decision was made by my camping companions to take me to a doctor, if we could find one.

We drove to the nearby resort, the Mangrove Hotel. Someone there gave us directions to the residence of a U. N. doctor who lived in the area. It took some searching in the driving rain, but we finally found the house described to us. Ronnie informed the sentry at the gate that we needed to see the doctor. It was late by that time, approaching 10 or 11 pm. The guard told us to wait in the doorway and a few minutes later, down the stairs and out the door came a Congolese woman who ran off into the night. We had heard rumors of the flexible morals of World Health personnel, so we shouldn't have been surprised. We looked at one another without speaking.

Our group was led upstairs into the residence. We entered a room that looked like something out of a novel or movie set: dim lights, a gigantic bar, big fireplace with elephant tusks on the mantle, drinks everywhere, the whole Hemingway bit.

As the little group of us drowned-rat Americans stepped into the room, two young Congolese women quietly entered the room from another doorway apparently to see who we were. They were each attired with only a bright colored African print cloth wrapped about them. From the look of their hair, wrappings and appearance we later speculated that we must have interrupted a Congo-style orgy of some kind.

A skinny, gray-haired man rose from a chair and greeted us, introducing himself as a U.N. doctor. He briefly quizzed me in broken English regarding my symptoms and announced confidently that I had a case of malaria. He retrieved some pills from his medical bag and after I consumed them with bottled water, drained in one thirsty gulp, we chatted briefly with the two other English-speaking U.N. men who were there.

The ladies of the night moved slowly about the room, sampling morsels from trays on the table and chatting quietly with the other occupants. Judging from their proximity and exchange of light touches the men and their lady friends were quite familiar with one another. We expressed our "Merci's" and "Au revoir's" before heading out into the driving rain and splashing our way back to our camp area.

It was a memorable evening that enriched both my immune system and my fantasy life; actually, the fantasy lives of us all.

It took a couple of days for my strength to fully return, but after the storm abated, we all were finally able to resume swimming in the surf and relaxing. We discovered that three other TASOK students had also come to the beach for spring break: Chris Rogers, Sandy Close and John Scott; but they had apparently had enough sense to stay in the resort hotel for the duration so they appeared to be in better shape than our group. They added to our raucous beach times and evening story telling.

We were pretty sandy, grimy and gross after a week of Congo camping but our small group remained in surprisingly good spirits. We found lots of things to laugh about and the mix of personalities was an entertaining and compatible one. Each was willing to do his part when help was needed. We shared the common bonds of adventure seeking and risk-taking, or was it just naiveté?

As the time neared for us to head back, we figured we'd had our excitement for the trip. It wasn't over quite yet, however.

Flipping flapjacks on the Muanda beach

27

Dogging the Military

"Life's challenges are not supposed to paralyze you, they're supposed to help you discover who you are."
— Bernice Johnson Reagon

We decided to head back to Kinshasa via a circuitous route and stop in for a visit with some other TASOK students at their home station, Kikonzi, a Christian & Missionary Alliance (C&MA) medical clinic. We had heard that it was a beautiful place and we *were* on holiday, after all, weren't we? The fact that Jimmy's girlfriend, Mimi, resided there had only a minor influence on the choice of our detour, or so he claimed.

It was a journey of nearly 100 miles northeast of the coast, into dense, jungle-like territory. The scenery was beautiful with steep hills, lush vegetation and palm oil plantations leading to deep forests with big trees, very unlike the dry grass, low brush, and rolling hills surrounding Kinshasa. Several things marred the beauty of the drive, however: all of them, military roadblocks. We had to stop at least a half-dozen times both coming and going to and from Kikonzi

The purpose of the numerous roadblocks was genuinely puzzling to us idealistic young men. At the time, we decided the military stopped us for two reasons: either the soldiers just wanted to look important and show their authority, or they wanted to hitch a ride to another location. Ron Weeks, our resident translator and cultural guide, did most of the talking at the various roadblocks.

When one policeman stopped us and just began to climb into our vehicle, Ron assured him that there was *surely* not enough room. Some 20 minutes of debate later, the policeman finally got out, slammed the door and angrily informed us, finger shaking in our direction, that if he ever saw us again, we'd be in big trouble – Lingala: *"mpashi mingi"*.

We were a bit concerned about this pronouncement, since he *was* headed in the same direction we were. At another stop, an army officer started to climb in our vehicle and Ronnie warned him that his dog, Rusty, was sometimes vicious, especially with Congolese. The fellow made a hasty retreat.

After all that creativity, our luck finally ran out. I inadvertently drove past a roadblock stop sign and then continued moving on the wrong side of a divider. Oops. In addition to my driving infractions, all five of us were grimy, unshaven, disheveled and dressed in nothing but shorts. We probably didn't smell very good either. Perhaps that's the real reason Rusty wanted to put his head out of the window when we drove. We made not the best of impressions.

After checking our papers, the military officer in charge of our checkpoint decided to send us with a guard to their army headquarters several kilometers away. At that point we figured we were in real trouble. We didn't know what to expect since we had heard stories of beatings and other adverse actions once soldiers took Westerners off the main highway.

The short conclusion to this anxious situation was that once we arrived at the army camp we were detained for only about 45 minutes, during which time the officer in charge rechecked our ID papers, gave us the third degree, told us we looked like "bandits" and then released us to continue on our way.

When we finally arrived at Kikonzi station by dark we were all physically and emotionally exhausted. A warm welcome from our hosts went a long way toward taking the edge off. That, and a big dinner. Ah, real food once again.

In spite of our interrupted arrival, my memories of our brief stay at Kikonzi are among my most positive of any locale in my entire sojourn in the Congo. It was a genuinely beautiful place. Everything was emerald green and there was a lovely stream gushing down from the nearby hills. Clean, whitewashed buildings were set in a large open area nestled in a cool setting with deep forest all around. Green grassy lawns sloped down to a stream with a small bridge leading to the hospital compound on the opposite hillside.

Dr. Neal Kroh and his wife, Esther, led the medical team at this C&MA post. Their children, twins Dave and Dan, plus younger sister, June, were students of mine at TASOK. I wasn't acquainted with their younger brother.

In the course of our visit, the Krohs took us to several small villages nearby. We were welcomed in a far different manner than we had become accustomed to as Westerners in the big city. People seemed curious and very interested in everything we did or said. As we drove through the forest roads, children ran behind our vehicle waving and calling out *"Mondele!"* We were assured by the Krohs that they had no concerns whatsoever about theft or violence; it simply didn't happen there. What a contrast to our experiences in Kinshasa!

Jimmy was able to spend time with his girlfriend, Mimi. In fact, we left him there in Kikonzi and he returned to TASOK a couple of days later with the group of missionary kids from that station.

The Krohs put us up in guest quarters they had on the station. We actually took showers, cold ones and slept in real beds during the two nights we stayed there. They were gracious hosts and it proved to be a wonderful conclusion to our spring break.

We ended our surfin' safari with a journey home animated by yet another series of roadblocks and cross-cultural encounters. With the practice we had had they seemed less daunting and somehow we managed to press on through one marathon day of driving to return back to Kinshasa.

I can't say that this was the most restful spring break I can remember, or that it was a particularly positive camping experience. It had to rank as my most memorable one, however. Subsequent bouts with malaria never failed to remind me of my surfin' safari on the Congo coast.

Postscript: Like many other experiences in this adventure the spring break camping and surfing trip I have described impacted me in a variety of subtle and enduring ways. Heading out over unknown and perilous roads with a certain confidence that somehow I would make it to my destination, relishing the experience along the way, proved to be an apt metaphor for *many* future voyages: vocational, recreational and even interpersonal. Marriage is one of the latter that comes to mind. My career path is yet another.

Finding personable and positive companions with whom to share one's adventures also seems a valuable life lesson. My early experiences in facing the threatening roadblocks of life with persistence, patience and a sense of humor became a perspective that has served me well over the years.

Finally, the capacity of our little group of young

men to appraise our varied experiences with a sense of appreciation, gratitude and awe is a spiritual quality that has been worthy of nurturing over a lifetime.

Surfin' safari team: Ron, Dave, Jimmy, John & Jim

28

Shifting Love Interests

"More important than the quest for certainty is the quest for clarity."

– Francois Gautier

E very good adventure has a little bit of romance. Mine was no exception. I certainly didn't plan it that way, however, as my first-meal denunciations illustrated at the Rempel dinner table the day we arrived in Kinshasa. Besides, my head and hands were completely filled with adaptations – new profession, new people, new climate, new everything. There wasn't much space in my head or heart for pursuing romantic thoughts, let alone *opportunity* to do so!

In the first weeks and months of my sojourn in Africa I continued to receive letters from my college girlfriend, Ann. I was pretty conflicted about receiving them. Fresh news from home, pictures, even music tapes she sent to me were welcome reminders of a meaningful life I had left behind. Ann and I had said our farewells and more-or-less agreed, as much as youth in their twenties are capable of doing, that our core values were not the same and would not sustain a future.

Ann was a good friend, a bright, attractive, quality person and I genuinely grieved the loss of her in my life, even though it was clear to me breaking up was the right thing to do. Thus, Ann's correspondence with me in Africa reopened the wound with each letter that arrived. I was flattered and delighted to receive her updates and to read how much I was missed. At the same time, I felt at a loss as to how to respond. Do I encourage these sentiments and reciprocate when I do not see a future to our relationship?

At one point, some months into the fall I finally decided I had to do the right thing. I wrote and indicated that I would need to notch-down the frequency of my replies since this was becoming just too difficult to continue. Ann's letters became fewer and the tone, less personal after that. In the spring of 1967 she finished her senior year at the U of O and ended up accepting a Peace Corps assignment in Ghana, West Africa after graduation.

"Hmmm. Congo is also in West Africa. Maybe?"

No. I chose not to open that door.

There were a few eligible American single gals in Kinshasa during my stint as a TASOK teacher. Some were USAID workers with the American embassy. My impression was that they were "well traveled" partiers and not in the same social world as we were. Others were short-term volunteers with different mission groups including MCC. Somehow the interests, personality or perspectives of these young women simply did not line up with mine. There were also several single women teachers at TASOK. They were nice people, but in most cases they were older than I and in every case, did not possess qualities that appealed in any way to my romantic interests.

One teacher who arrived on the scene, Arlene, initially seemed to be someone with whom I might build a friendship. She had been a competitive women's tennis player in college. Sometime soon after her arrival we arranged a friendly game of tennis. At that time, I still thought of myself as an athlete. Even though my tennis playing was strictly amateur, I was competitive in my approach to recreation and was often successful in tennis matches with peers. I guess Arlene decided she should impress me with her tennis prowess in that first encounter. It was not a good decision, at least not from *my perspective*, anyhow.

As Arlene "killed" her serves, one after another, she also killed her chances of building a relationship with me. She broke my best game and shattered my surprisingly fragile male ego all in one warm, humid afternoon game of tennis. It proved to be a symbolic, though completely effective "turn off." In subsequent encounters, never again on a tennis court, I concluded that interpersonal finesse was likely not Arlene's best game. I was uninterested in pursuing this friendship any more seriously, on or off a tennis court.

In contrast to Arlene's assertive, even aggressive strategy of relating to me, demure high school senior, Betty Jean Rempel, was friendly, reserved and respectful in her periodic contacts with me. It was to be expected, I suppose, since I *was* a teacher, after all, and she was a student, though not in any of my classes.

BJ and I had initially met in her home on my first day in the Congo and subsequently our paths crossed at the English-speaking church, occasionally at TASOK and more often at the afternoon siesta hour swim at the Athénée Royale pool. This setting served as a weekly informal gathering of English-speaking young adults in Kinshasa. While I had few one-on-one conversations with her, Betty Jean's youthful beauty, maturity and poise caught my attention. I began to notice whether or not she was there when I arrived at the pool.

One afternoon, several of us young men tried some fancy dives off the board, showing off to an appreciative audience of young guys and gals and soaking up their cheers and laughter as we either made or miserably failed in our diving contortions. I tried a "coup de pied à la lune" – rough translation: "kick at the moon" – dive, failed to unfold in time and hit the water hard with my knee smashing into my forehead. It split my right eyebrow and I bled like a stuck pig, with my eye instantly swelling shut.

Fortunately, help was near. BJ rushed to my aid, located a cloth to stop the bleeding and contacted someone to arrange for a ride to a doctor. My split eyebrow required five stitches and I had an impressive shiner for days afterwards. I also had BJ's full attention. Her follow up inquiries and teasing were welcome, if unintended consequences of my face smash.

Betty Jean began to have *my* attention as well. I was first impressed that she hit home runs over the chicken coup near the softball field. She was a good athlete. BJ served as the regular organist for the 500 + English-speaking Protestant Church. She accompanied special music on the piano and sometimes sang and played the vibraharp. She played the clarinet in the high school band and participated in that year's musical, "South Pacific." She was a talented musician. Betty Jean was a cheerleader, the editor of the school's annual, and a straight-A student, ending the year as valedictorian of her graduating class. She was an intelligent and personable young woman.

I began to pay attention when in casual conversation others referenced BJ's qualities. Her English teacher, Faith Nickel, viewed her as academically the most promising of her class; my roommate, Jim, told me about her creative and clever presentations in his speech class; my principal's wife, Ruby, informed me how impressed she was at all the things BJ's mom had taught her to do: music, food preparation, sewing, organizing and planning. "I don't think there is *anything* those Rempel girls can't do!"

As attractive and talented as she was, my interest being piqued, I didn't have much of a personal relationship with Betty Jean at that point.

That was about to change, however.

29

A Bit of Romance

"No, there's nothing half so sweet in life as love's young dream."
    – Thomas Moore

I t was May, just a few weeks before the end of the school year. In one poolside conversation, BJ informed me that there was a tennis court on the British Baptist Mission grounds near her house.

"Would you like to play tennis sometime?"

Would I! After our hastily arranged tennis game, which she must have let me win, we walked to her house. We sat outside, ate homemade cinnamon buns, drank ice tea and visited about all kinds of topics that were apparently unprocessed in her mind to that point.

Betty Jean had lots of questions about spiritual issues, concerns about her college choice, and anxiety about leaving home in the Congo. I was flattered and delighted to engage in conversation on these meaningful topics. Her depth of character impressed me.

Unseen by me, Betty Jean's mother silently and skeptically watched us from the window.

BJ reported later that her mom had quizzed her, "What in the world did you have to talk about with that man?"

"*God*," was Betty Jean's succinct and slightly smug reply.

By that time, I *was* becoming interested and attracted to this capable young lady. I kept running scenarios over in my mind, trying to imagine her in my home setting. Would I notice her qualities and develop a friendship if we were both living in Eugene, Oregon? Would I still be interested in someone five years younger? Was it just being in Africa with a limited range of eligibles that prompted my interest in BJ?

Somehow I just couldn't process these thoughts to conclusion, but neither could I ignore a genuine interest that had been slowly but surely captivated. One thing was certain: I wasn't about to say anything to my parents. Doing so would trigger a flood of concern and advice that would be as unhelpful as it would be unwelcome. My father's warning words were still with me.

I did share my sentiments with my roommate, Jim, however. He happened to be briefly hospitalized at that time for eradication of some sort of intestinal parasite. He shared a hospital room with one of BJ's high school classmates, so I had to be quiet and discreet in my comments.

I told Jim I was thinking – actually, praying – that if BJ showed up at the Athénée pool that very afternoon, *that* would be my "sign" to ask her out for an actual *date*. TASOK graduation had just taken place, so it would technically meet my standard of not dating a high school student. Jim seemed delighted and intrigued by the venture, in spite of being drugged and feeling really lousy.

"Go for it," he encouraged, "but you *have to* let me know what happens, in detail."

BJ was at the pool. The movie, "War and Peace", a 1956 Henry Fonda, Audrey Hepburn, Mel Ferrer classic from the Leo Tolstoy novel, dubbed in French, was showing in town. I asked to take her to the show. She accepted with no hesitation.

"Don't you need to check with your parents?" I asked, wondering if I would run into opposition.

"Yes, but I'm sure it will be OK," was her reply.

My memories of that first official date are mostly colored by the events at the end of the evening. That's when the fireworks went off. I do remember that we parked and walked a couple of blocks to the theatre. I grasped Betty Jean's hand as we crossed the street and she held on tight.

The movie was almost three and a half hours in length. That's *forever* when the dialog is in French and you can't understand a word of the language. The action scenes were spectacular and it was nice sitting next to my lovely date, who occasionally translated for me.

We again held hands returning to the car and I drove her back to her home.

BJ's high school senior photo

BJ's parents were asleep, or being very quiet, when we arrived at her home. We retreated to the kitchen where we decided to make a late night omelet. Preparing food seemed like a good way to prolong the evening. It was nearly midnight by the time we ate, visiting first about the movie and then about her imminent departure for the states and summer school at Wheaton College.

As the time arrived for me to leave, we entered the

hallway. I turned to Betty Jean and pulling her close, kissed her.

What comes to mind at this point is a line from the 1987 movie, *The Princess Bride*: *"Since the invention of the kiss there have been five kisses that were rated the most passionate, the most pure. This one left them all behind."*

BJ and I had two additional "dates" in the week that remained before her departure for college in Illinois. We went to a "Wild West" production one evening at a local equestrian club. There were a number of other members of the TASOK community there and I'm sure some eyebrows were raised when we showed up together, though I wasn't paying attention.

We also took a drive a day or so later to a scenic lake just outside of the city, "Lac de Ma Vallée." At one point BJ climbed a big anthill while I stood watching. She jumped off into my arms and I kissed her once again. It seemed pretty romantic at the time. It wasn't the ants that were stirred up. Romantic, perhaps, but also *improbable*. Who knew where this attraction might lead? BJ was scheduled to leave the country in just two days to start a new chapter in her life and I had another year of service in Africa.

Two days later Jim and I found ourselves driving to the Ndjili Airport to see Betty Jean and several of her classmates off for the States. I had no idea what I would say to her but I knew I didn't want to miss saying farewell in person. The students stood around in the airport lobby in small groups of family and friends, making small talk, recalling good times together and waiting for the final departure call. Jim and I chatted with different students and I edged closer to BJ's circle of supporters.

When the boarding call finally came for her international flight, BJ smiled and turned toward me, moving a couple of steps away from her parents and friends. I quietly said to her, "I'm going to miss you, Betty Jean." I had decided I would be bold and at least give her a goodbye hug.

"Me too," she said with tears in her eyes and reached up and *kissed me*, on the mouth!

She then turned to Jim and shook his hand "Goodbye Mr. Becker," she said, before waving to her parents, and quickly, tearfully following her classmates out the door to the plane.

I was flattered and thrilled but aghast! *What* had just happened? I was afraid to look around to see what kind of reactions that goodbye solicited from the TASOK community that was present, including BJ's parents. Jim looked at me with a big grin on his face.

"Well! *That* was some farewell."

As we drove back to our apartment we discussed the incident. Jim reported that there were a lot of surprised people in the airport that afternoon. "Shocked" was his actual descriptor.

"So what does this mean for the two of you?" he asked.

"I have no idea," was my reply, but I knew in my heart that somehow my life would never be the same.

30

A First Piece of Pai

"The journey between what you once were and who you are now becoming is where the dance of life really takes place."
– Barbara Deangelis

One of the ways that transformation takes place in people's lives, I have observed, is when their usual supports and identity are in some dramatic fashion, stripped away. Sometimes this happens because of illness, accident or injury; other times, the precipitants are circumstantial like a sudden job loss or being stranded on a desert island. My six-week sojourn in the tiny rural Congo settlement of Pai Kongila served as *my* transformational stimulus in the summer of 1967.

Personal transformation is a recognizable process. For most people it begins with facing a significant challenge. This may initiate a sense of discomfort, present a set of obstacles and evolve to become a full-blown threat or even a crisis. The "challenge," of whatever character, involves exposure to something that we cannot easily grasp and overcome, or is something so potentially dangerous, so novel, or so at-odds with our life experience that we begin feeling overwhelmed.

Most people respond to large-scale threats at least initially with resistance. We tell ourselves that we are not going to permit ourselves be overwhelmed by the impinging circumstances! However, when it becomes obvious that resistance is futile, *that's* when personal transformation *really* begins. We then refocus our energies and accept deep down inside that our previous ways of being, doing and living will no longer serve us successfully. We begin to explore in earnest, new possibilities, even as we step away from the patterns of thinking and operating that may have served us well in the past.

My experience in Pai Kongila triggered this process in my life.

I landed in the tiny middle-of-nowhere village through a strange turn of events. Our first year of teaching at TASOK had drawn to a close and the summer opened before us. It was unclear what the Christian Service program expected of teachers during the summer holidays, especially those of us who were concurrently fulfilling our Selective Service obligations to the U.S. government. Most of the non-alternate-service teachers left Kinshasa to travel in Europe or to visit their stateside home and family.

Our adventures in voyaging to this African teaching assignment had only stimulated the travel bug in

Jim and me. After many informal conversations with other young adult peers, we formulated a summer plan. Note: I am using the word "plan" pretty loosely. Here's what it entailed: we would fly on Air Congo to Goma on the east side of the country, hitchhike on big commercial trucks the short distance into Uganda and then connect with East African Railways and tour Uganda, Kenya and Tanzania for five weeks before returning to the Congo a week or two before the start of school.

Before we headed out on this ill-conceived fantasy trip, we decided we'd better cover any potential criticism of our "plan" with two or three weeks of voluntary service. After all, we reasoned, those in military service wouldn't be able to just take an entire summer off.

A little investigation among local missionary contacts yielded a good possibility. Jake Nickel, a civil engineer with the Mennonite Brethren Missions & Services, was in need of help in constructing a big water tank in a remote setting that included a small medical clinic and several missionary-occupied residences near a tiny native village.

Pai Kongila was located in grassy steppe country nearly 300 miles southeast of Kinshasa. The nearest water supply was a small stream at the base of a deep canyon. Jake had engineered a pipeline and pump to bring the precious liquid up to the top of the plateau where the clinic was located and where people resided. Constructing a water storage tank out of heavy metal plates, abandoned by the Belgians at Congo's independence, would thus be a huge benefit to the members of this rural community, especially those dispensing medical services.

This project sounded like something Jim and I could manage. We proceeded to make the necessary arrangements with the missionaries on site, with MAF to fly us there and pick us back up in 16 days and we packed our bags. It was the third week of June 1967.

Our two-hour MAF flight from Kinshasa to Pai Kongila was exciting. It was the first flight in a small aircraft for Jim and me and the pilot's maneuverings of the plane and commentary en route were fascinating for both of us. After a couple of circles around the landing zone to alert the locals of our arrival we touched down on the roughly cleared field.

Greeting committee at the Pai Kongila landing strip

Touched down? It would be far more accurate to say we bounced and lurched along the runway that had apparently not been well cleared and leveled via the directives of the local village chief. Our pilot sighed, "That's got to be fixed!"

A small crowd of curious children and villagers were present to welcome us, as were several of the missionaries who lived at this location. Three Canadian couples, with two young children each and three single nurses constituted the entire white population of Pai Kongila at that time.

Pai Kongila seemed like the end of the earth. In our dusty walk from the field that served as the MAF landing zone, we noticed how dry and bleak everything appeared. The few bushes and occasional tree seemed stunted, thirsty and the grassy roadsides were parched and golden.

We carried our luggage to the doctor's residence, since his dwelling had a screened porch that would serve as our bedroom. The missionary group had arranged to have us two fellows rotate to a different home each day for meals so that we would not deplete the larders of any one household.

There was no electricity; kerosene lamps provided dim evening illumination. Each missionary house had an indoor bathroom, but no running water, the reason for constructing the storage tank. Each person was allocated one five pound Maxwell House coffee can full of water to use for a daily bath. Afterwards, we were instructed to scoop up as much dirty bath water as we could from the tub and place it in the toilet tank, which was flushed once daily for the entire household.

Pai Kongila needed a water tank, all right.

Jim and I soon settled into a new kind of daily routine. We worked on constructing the storage tank in the mornings and resumed our duties once again after our noon meal and rest. Jake had a crew of local Congolese men who assisted as well. They were so slight of stature that it took several of us to wrestle each of the heavy four by four foot metal plates in place.

As isolated as Jim and I felt, we became very interested in snippets of news that came from the daily short wave radio transmissions between area mission stations and from BBC World News received on the short wave radio at supper time.

Sleeping was a new challenge because of the critters that regularly invaded our bed space after dark. They were mostly big flying cockroaches and occasional crickets and centipedes. I ended up leaving a lamp lit each night since it limited the entry of the annoying bugs until I fell asleep. The lamp eventually burned down and extinguished.

The one concession to all of this strangeness was that Jim and I at least had one another with whom to share our observations, anxieties, frustrations and bewilderments. But that also came to an end.

For a whole, two long weeks we nobly endured our perceived hardships as if they were some kind of merit

badge in missionary living. We did so by telling ourselves that a person could put up with nearly *anything*
for a short time. Nevertheless, we privately counted off
the days until we could return to civilization, Kinshasa,
and get on with our lives and our summer plans. Our
hosts were remarkably upbeat and we were genuinely impressed that *they* did not dwell on what they
didn't have: conveniences, cleanliness, and distractions/
entertainment.

Life for the local Congolese, however, was pretty
grim. The children mostly had red hair from lack of
protein in their diet. What protein was consumed by
locals consisted of occasional snakes or rats shot with
short bows and arrows. Patients in the clinic had to
have friends or relatives camp outside the building
and cook for them, since there was no food service.
We white folks must have appeared to be rich beyond
comprehension to the desperately impoverished locals.
Talk about putting "hardship" into perspective!

Jim and I reacted to our circumstances just like any
self-respecting *tourist* might. We were sympathetic to
the plight of both local Congolese and missionaries, but
bottom-line thankful that we didn't have to share their
misery for long. It would make a good story someday,
we thought.

Events shortly overtook us that made this reflection
a prediction.

31
Unexpectedly On My Own

"You only grow when you are alone."
    – Paul Newman

W ith just days left before our return to Kinshasa, Jim came down with another serious bout of intestinal parasites. It may have come from eating local dishes associated with the 30th of June Congo Independence celebration we attended as special guests. Whatever the source, he was pretty sick and needed some powerful medications available only in the big city.

Two days prior to our scheduled return flight, a small plane unexpectedly appeared overhead while Jake and I were at the tank project. It buzzed low over the area to signal intent to land before setting down. The MAF pilot had flown to another mission station in the area but then decided to detour to Pai Kongila, unannounced, to drop off some mail.

On short notice, Neil Voth, Pai's MCC doctor, proposed that Jim return *on this flight* so that he could get to the medications he needed ASAP. I should plan to pack up our things and follow in two days on our scheduled MAF return flight, or so Dr. Voth suggested. Jim took a small, hastily packed bag, climbed in and the plane departed as abruptly as it had arrived. No problem losing my partner, it would only be for a couple of days.

What happened next shook our little mission station to the core. The following day, July 5, 1967, a Belgian by the name of Jean Schramme, led approximately 100 fellow mercenaries and 1,000 Katangese soldiers in rebelling against the Congo government. This was known as the Second Kisangani Mutiny or the Mercenaries Mutiny. The rebels intended to secede the mineral rich Eastern part of the country from the rest of the volatile African nation. Their action resulted in a *huge* national crisis, which directly affected even us in our remote location.

All flights to and within the Congo were grounded: no MAF return flight, no letters from home or from Betty Jean. All whites, including the small group of us in Pai Kongila, were placed on a dusk to dawn curfew. In addition, all radios were confiscated from Europeans: no short wave connections. The local military also initially confiscated one of our three mission vehicles and gasoline, purportedly to use to "patrol for mercenaries."

Note: the rebellion was approximately 1,000 miles distance from Pai Kongila. No matter that it was virtually impossible that any mercenaries would ever pass by our region. What this development meant to *me* was that I was stranded at the end of the earth for an indeterminate period, under curfew, out of touch with the outside world and emotionally isolated from family and friends.

In the first days that followed the curfew I felt as lost and lonely as I ever have, before or since. All that connected me to the real world had been stripped away. Not knowing the native tongue, there was no communicating with the local populace. Everything felt temporary or provisional. Completely dependent on my hosts, I was passed from one home to another for meals. They had their spouses or partners with whom to process; I was alone.

It was all very unsettling. Just three years earlier in a previous Congo uprising, Western missionaries had been killed. Would *we* be subject to deadly threats? How would we know what was evolving in this rebellion, with no radio? How would we ever escape with no vehicles?

I realized that as long as Jim had been with me, the two of us had denied or minimized our awkwardness and dependency. Now I had to face myself in a way I had not imagined ever doing. I did a lot of praying with an earnestness that was as intense as it was new to me.

I should clarify, however, that *my* fears and anxieties about the crisis situation, the isolation and the potential threat of local military authorities was *not* shared by all of my missionary hosts. Helen Nickel described their family's sentiments to me years later in the following correspondence:

"We actually felt quite safe because the army was camped right behind our house and they were very protective. The curfew was a bit uncomfortable because at times the soldiers would walk around the house usually at night. I don't know if they did that to every house. The insecure feeling of not knowing whether we would be able to stay or not or how would we get out added to the instability of our presence there. But I must say that the people there were very protective and the church prayed constantly. Local Congolese Pastor Bernard was an amazing leader in the area of faith and praying was first on his list. I think we felt a lot less safe in Kinshasa than we did in Pai, believe it or not."

As distressing as these circumstances seemed, they did prompt a focus on the here-and-now instead of the future. I began to find some evidence of character strength hidden underneath my young adult surface persona. Perhaps my inner self, exposed by these circumstances, was more fluid and adaptable than I had imagined.

John & fellow workers at Pai water tank

32

Ending a Non-Career

"A man cannot be comfortable without his own approval"
– Mark Twain

I can remember very clearly just when things began to turn around for me. It was at that very moment I began to own my adult life and choices.

At some point in my stay at Pai Kongila, I had informed Dr. Voth that my college major was Pre-Med. He naturally expressed interest and asked if I intended to follow up my alternate service stint with an application to medical school. I informed him that I had a lot of ambivalence about a medical career. He offered to have me assist him in surgery to help me test out my interest in this field.

The next day, instead of working with Jake, I accompanied Neil Voth to the clinic. His surgery of the day was a cesarean birth. The operating room was a small enclosure with open, screened windows on two sides. The gurney in the center occupied most of the space. The surgery was hot, stuffy, smelling of disinfectant and blood. One of Dr. Voth's Congolese nurses moved about the room swatting flies while a second nurse assisted him in surgery. We each had a surgical mask over our mouths and noses. I immediately felt light-headed and nauseous.

As Neil prepared a very pregnant African patient for her cesarean incision, he explained that this procedure was necessary because the little girl who was his patient was just too young – ten or twelve at most – to successfully deliver via natural childbirth. The small stature of the girl seemed to accentuate the size of her distended belly. Until he administered the anesthesia, the patient moaned and cried. I was beginning to feel a bit overwhelmed by the entire scene.

Dr. Voth then made an incision and blood and water gushed out of the patient's tightly stretched belly. I sat down quickly and put my head between my legs to keep from fainting and totally humiliating myself. Neil then pulled out a tiny gray life form and with a swat, it turned into a crying baby.

That was my epiphany moment.

At that instant, as clear as neon flashing on my conscious mind, the thought came to me: "I don't have to do this! If being a doctor means liking this kind of stuff, I'm *done* with this career!" What else might I do with my life? That question was quite unclear at the moment. What *was* clear, however, from that point on was that it *wouldn't* be pursuing a medical career.

Psychologist Jack Mezirow labels this process of changing one's thinking, *"perspective transformation."* It occurs when one is confronted with a disorienting dilemma, that is, a set of circumstances that causes one to critically reflect on previously held assumptions and beliefs. One then consciously makes plans and discovers new ways to define and view one's world. A former perspective is replaced with a new one that is more open, flexible and valid.

In my case, isolation at Pai Kongila and direct exposure to Dr. Voth's surgery provided the stimulus for disrupting my former career ideas. Admittedly, I had entertained serious doubts about medicine as a future objective, but I still needed to work through my ambivalence and open myself up to other, more appropriate possibilities.

I believe that's just what happened on the morning I have described.

Postscript: Once I was able to stand up again without fainting, I informed Dr. Voth that my career exploration would *not* require more time in his operating room. I actually departed the clinic with a new lightness to my step.

33

The Last Piece of Pai

---

*"If you see oppression of the poor, and justice and
righteousness trampled in a country, do not be astounded."*
– King Solomon, Eccl. 5:8

A s remote and isolated as my unexpected exile
was, there seemed to be no shortage of opportunities for learning and growth– emotionally, spiritually
and culturally – in the restricted circumstances I faced.
I decided to make the best of my limited options and to
absorb what I could while I was there.

One of the Canadian missionaries in our little
community, Jake Penner, had a literature distribution
assignment. Not sure what that meant or how effective
it might be in a region with few schools and presumably
an illiterate population, I asked if I might accompany
him on his next outreach to villages in the region.

"This should be a learning experience," I figured.

Jake eagerly agreed, pleased to have my interest and

company. He determined that we had better head out soon, however, since he reasoned, correctly, that the local military authorities were likely to return any time to appropriate his vehicle. That would end any further village literature distribution visits. We planned to head out the next day.

Our target? Two villages located over two hours away on back roads near an abandoned Belgian palm oil plantation. Jake had not made it that far in his distribution efforts to date and he understood that it was a location seldom visited by Europeans. "Nearly untouched by the gospel," were his words as his eyes lit up in excitement. "An ideal place to plant some seeds."

The *seeds* presumably referred to the Gospel message in the liberally illustrated gospel tracts he had packed in boxes in his house.

We set out on the deeply rutted, dusty roads the next morning in the company of a small wiry Congolese pastor named Bernard, our lunch, some water and several boxes of tracts rattling around in the back of a creaky old gray Chevy van. Oh yes, we were also equipped with an ample supply of Jake's optimism.

A brief aside is appropriate here. I did not realize at the time that I was in the presence of a contemporary "hero of faith" in the Congolese Mennonite Brethren church. The diminutive cleric accompanying us was none other than Pastor Bernard Kasai, whose Christian witness was referenced many times in the missionary community during my stay in Congo. John B. Toews recounts his story in a 1978 book, *The Mennonite Brethren Church in Zaire.*

During the 1964 "Simba rebellion" in the Stanleyville-Kivu area many Christians, especially the church leaders, were persecuted for their faith. The rebels stopped an assistant pastor from the area, Bernard Kasai, while he was attempting to get his family to safety. They demanded that he dig a grave for himself. "We shall not hear your preaching again. That we will end," they told him.

Toews picks up the tale at that point:

"With much difficulty he dug a grave with a hoe that was handed to him. The grave completed, he was asked to kneel while the soldiers shoveled the earth back into the hole. When the dirt came up to his shoulders, the rebels began arguing among themselves. Some wanted to finish the job, kill him and close the grave completely. Others, even though they bore the name "rebel," were quite a different brand. Some of them were Kasai's former Sunday school pupils. They felt for him and resisted covering his head with earth. After a lengthy argument they left him, still buried up to his neck.

Three days later, having received permission from the local rebel commander, one of the former Sunday school students returned. Finding Kasai still alive, he went down on his knees and clawed away the dirt.

"Now run," he whispered. At first Kasai's cramped muscles refused to move, but gradually he was able to move his muscles. With much difficulty he reached the hiding place of his family. God spared Kasai's life for a ministry which he is continuing today (1978)."

John with pastor Bernard & soldier distributing literature

I had no clue that I was in the presence of this legendary believer. I perceived at the time that Pastor Bernard was a quietly confident diminutive Congolese Christian colleague and partner in the day's activities who seemed very much at home in his skin. Throughout our day together he did not appear alarmed or distressed at any of the events we witnessed. In retrospect, I wish I had had the language capacity to dialog with

Pastor Bernard at the time. It's obvious this "tested believer" had much to offer to us sheltered Westerners.

We had barely left the settlement of Pai Kongila
before we came to our first military roadblock. The arrival of our van generated not only a cloud of dust but
also a great deal of excitement for the bored, previously lethargic soldiers. Imagine, an actual vehicle to stop
and one containing two *white men*, no less! The reason
for the roadblock was reportedly to stop mercenaries
and their conspirators.

The uniformed guards jumped up, grabbed their
guns, ordered us out and barked a number of loud directives that I couldn't understand. Jake, a short, bow-legged,
stocky man, was not impressed. He was not about to be
intimidated by these characters. After a brief exchange,
with Jake and Pastor Bernard taking charge of the situation, the soldiers quickly backed off. Jake smiled, handed
each man a gospel tract and we drove on.

This experience was repeated two more times in the
next hour, a process I found no less alarming with each
stop. At the third roadblock a longer set of negotiations
took place. Jake and Pastor Bernard identified the purpose of our trip, explaining that we "Mondeles" were
missionaries. The soldiers were then offered tracts. At
length, the officer in charge indicated he would permit
us to continue on only if he could send along an armed
soldier. Jake reluctantly agreed. The *four* of us then
continued on our hot, bumpy journey until we finally
came to the first of the two villages Jake had targeted.

It's difficult to accurately portray how bleak and dirty things were at that remote settlement. It was unlike anything I had seen or imagined as a dwelling place for humans. The huts were positioned in a long row, on either side of a central path or street that stretched for over half a kilometer. Each residence consisted of mud plastered on sticks, crumbling with a poorly thatched roof. Few huts had any windows, so they were quite dark. Children ran about completely naked and the bare-breasted village women had orange-red mud plastered over their hair and upper bodies. Jake thought the purpose was to ward off insect bites.

Proud village mama & child

Our arrival generated high excitement. The children squealed and pointed and the entire village population gathered about our van. After greeting the elders, pastor Bernard explained we had information about God to give to them. This was Catholic territory so he was not allowed to preach. We *were* allowed to walk down the street and place literature in each hut, however. The elders offered us some palm wine. The soldier accepted, but Jake and pastor Bernard declined. I followed their lead. After we finished distributing the tracts we drove off. A cloud of dust and cheering children accompanied our vehicle's departure.

I was impressed. That seemed to go very well. People were eager to receive the religious materials. We shared our lunch with our companions, the pastor and soldier and drove three or four kilometers to the next village. Much like the last one, this pathetically impoverished settlement had likely not seen a white man for years. We began to distribute literature as before, accompanied by a growing crowd of curious villagers as we walked down the kilometer-long street. But this time, Jake and Pastor Bernard had not first asked for permission. This was a mistake.

By the time we finished our rounds, a large crowd of noisy, excited mud-caked men, women and children had surrounded our vehicle. The little pastor briefly spoke to them, presumably about the purpose of our visit. This time his speech was greeted with some jeers and heckling as the crowd became even more agitated, pushing and pressing us against the vehicle, demanding more materials, food, "*Cadeaux*" (gifts).

As the tension increased, our armed traveling partner suddenly stepped forward and with a dramatic flourish, clicked the bolt to cock his rifle. I have no idea if it contained any ammunition but it certainly got the attention of the crowd. The villagers scattered in an instant with squeals of alarm. Jake and his pastor partner then had an overdue conversation with the miffed village elders, apologizing for their error of protocol.

What a curious juxtaposition, I thought: a pacifist Mennonite and a Congolese pastor distributing gospel tracts with the help of an armed soldier. Could missionary work get any stranger than that?

My final lesson of the day was by far the most traumatic. It heightened my sense of vulnerability and horrified me as I witnessed an abusive exercise in power and oppression animated by senseless violence. I had not ever imagined people were capable of such things.

Returning from the villages, we arrived back once again at the third roadblock where our soldier/passenger exited. As we drove up, the small group of his military buddies was gathered around the crumpled heap of a man dressed in bloody rags. Each soldier took his turn hitting and kicking the pitiful fellow who was curled up on the ground. The man's eyes were swollen shut and he looked close to death, moaning, barely moving. When we inquired as to the fellow's crime, the soldiers indicated he did not have "proper papers."

The soldier in charge then motioned for us to leave. *"Kwenda!"* It was an order, not a suggestion. He was not entertaining further questions. Shaken, we slowly drove away.

In fact, the soldiers had been drinking, were bored and I believe the unfortunate victim just served as the afternoon's entertainment. As far removed from everything and everyone as we were, it wasn't hard to imagine how easy it might have been for the soldiers to direct the same fate *our* way. My memories of this graphic incident haunted my dreams for months afterwards.

This day's experience heightened for me not only how privileged I was but also how vulnerable. I had not ever imagined that humans could subsist in such difficult and deprived conditions. I also had never realized how easily the bullies of the world could dominate and control common people.

These were unexpectedly valuable lessons in the reality of oppression.

34

Escaping Isolation

"The only certain freedom is in departure"
– Robert Frost

A few days after our village literature distribution experience, the old, gray Chevy van was indeed confiscated by the local authorities. At that point, I assisted my host, Dr. Voth, in burying a ten-liter can of gasoline behind his house as an emergency reserve. His white Willys Jeep station wagon was the sole remaining vehicle at the site to eventually evacuate all of us Caucasian residents.

Later that week, I lingered a bit longer than usual after dinner with the Penners, listening to the BBC on their short wave radio. They had managed to stash a radio away when the military appropriated electronic devices from Westerners in the area. We were told that the soldiers even took a nearby Belgian priest's *hearing aid* away, thinking it might be a device to call in mercenaries.

We were all quite concerned with the BBC's reports of the status of the rebellion. Apparently, the 1,100-man rebel force was managing to hold its own against 32,000 soldiers in the national army. No early end to the country's crisis was predicted.

At the end of the news report I headed out from the Penners' toward the Voth's house where I slept. It was about a half kilometer away. The moonless night was as dark as a closed closet at midnight, though it was only just after seven PM at the time. I had not thought to bring a flashlight, so I made my way along slowly, stumbling down the dusty rutted road all the time keeping the dim kerosene light of the distant Voth house in sight.

All of a sudden, breaking the stillness of the night I heard in the distance the sound of a vehicle banging its way up the hilly road leading to Pai Kongila. Panic seized me as I realized that it was a military patrol – perhaps more of a "joy ride" than a patrol – and walking along in the dark, I was in violation of the national curfew for Westerners. Moreover, I couldn't communicate with my captors should I be stopped. I was not on the privileged side of racial profiling here. With the horrific beating I had witnessed still fresh in mind and no place to hide, I did the only thing I could think of and started running for my life!

The banging van with lights bouncing up and down grew ever closer, headed in the direction of our residences. By that time I was running flat-out in the pitch-black night aiming for the Voth's. My all-out sprint surely could have been a new Olympic record, had there only been a timer handy. It ended abruptly. *Wham!*

I hit the object at full stride. I flew in a summersault through the air, landing in a heap on my back. It was a Mobylette motorbike parked in front of the nurses' residence in the dark.

As I lay there, the patrol van turned only twenty yards from me and pulled up behind the missionary nurses' house, where several female Congolese student nurses lived. Apparently, it was just a social call that evening, not a search and capture mission.

I gathered myself up and limped on the last hundred yards to the Voths who patched the gash in my shin and assured me that I had not broken my leg. I was *very* shaken. It felt like a bad nightmare.

A few days later even the Willys Jeep was in jeopardy. Apparently, the local military had crashed or otherwise rendered inoperable both of the vehicles they had previously appropriated from the missionaries at Pai. The grey Chevy van that had chased me home was the last to die. Now, a local military leader, in full uniform, beret cocked to one side of his head, marched stiffly to the porch of Dr. Voth, accompanied by two aides armed with banana clip rifles. He banged on the door. They were there to confiscate Dr. Voth's station wagon.

I joined the serious group in the Voth's living room

and sat through the long and tense meeting between the Colonel – was that his rank? – and Neil Voth. I was clearly able to absorb the angry tenor of the exchanges though I could not understand the words, spoken in French and Kituba. The two accompanying soldiers sat stiffly at attention with their rifles on their laps.

At one point, the ammunition clip fell from one of the seated soldier's guns and his bullets rolled across the tile floor. The Colonel glanced over, annoyed. The soldier hastily jammed the bullets back into the clip and stuffed it back into his rifle. A couple of minutes later the very same thing happened a second time and the shamed soldier repeated his hurried correction. In his haste, however, he jammed the bullets back into the clip but they were facing both directions. I imagined he'd likely blow his head off if he discharged his weapon.

The absurdity and tension of the moment put me on the verge of laughter. I bit my tongue until I tasted blood.

Finally, as the tone and volume of exchanges escalated, Neil leaned forward pointing his finger toward the officer. He slowly and deliberately made his point. A few awkward moments of silence followed as the Colonel absorbed Neil's message. Then, he slowly rose, squared his shoulders, turned on his heel and strode out of the house, his two armed henchmen following with as much military dignity as they had left to display.

What had just happened? Neil did not want to talk. He abruptly headed out the door for the clinic with an angry scowl on his face. His wife, Helga, then graciously explained to me what had just transpired. The Colonel was indeed putting pressure on Neil to give up the station's last remaining vehicle. Neil had refused. The Colonel made threats. Neil had countered, saying that if he proceeded to commandeer the vehicle and if subsequent to that action, he or any of his wives, children or members of his family or tribe became ill, Neil and his medical staff would simply not lift a finger to help. Since there were no other medical resources for many kilometers in any direction, this provided an effective halt to the Colonel's demand.

Now, I'd like to imagine that this dedicated missionary doctor would not have *actually* held out as described, if tested, but in that little afternoon "poker match" Dr. Voth's bluff worked. I'll bet *those details* weren't part of any church deputation report, however.

. . . .

On a Monday, almost three weeks after the mercenary rebellion began, MBMS missionary John Ratzlaff arrived in Pai Kongila, unannounced on a commercial truck. We were delighted and greatly relieved to see him. He had two items of good news: 1) The Congo military was now allowing some movement by commercial vehicles and mission personnel and 2) Air Congo had resumed flights from Kikwit, the nearest city, to Kinshasa. The mission administration was therefore urging MBMS personnel to evacuate rural assignments and head for the cities.

Note: The Pai Kongila missionaries had months previously made flight reservations to Kinshasa for that very next Wednesday, to attend their yearly retreat. After pumping Ratzlaff for further news, we hastily packed for our trip to Kikwit and then hopefully, on to Kinshasa.

Our prior efforts to safeguard gasoline and Neil's resistance to giving up the station's last vehicle were duly rewarded as we pulled out from Pai Kongila the next morning crowded into his white Willys Jeep.

They say missions' work brings people together. Well, we were *very together*, all right, ten of us, including Ratzlaff and our luggage were crammed into that station wagon. It took us seven hours to traverse the 110 kilometers to Kikwit. Usually the trip took three or four hours but Dr. Voth had insisted that we drive slowly because Helen Nickel was several months pregnant and could experience complications from a rough ride.

During the long, slow, bumpy drive I thus worried about a new catastrophe. Compulsively, every few minutes I queried my pregnant seatmate, "How are you doing?" as we bounced along the deeply rutted road. Annoying! The patient Helen finally told me kindly but firmly, "Stop, John. I'll let everyone know if I'm having any difficulty." We passed through several military roadblocks without major incident. We finally came into Kikwit, but we arrived after the Air Congo offices had closed. It appeared that we'd have to take our chances at purchasing our tickets at the airport in the morning.

At 8:30 AM the next day, the scheduled time of departure, the local airport officials insisted they would not allow us to board the flight without tickets purchased from the mid-town offices 20 minutes away! Missionary Archie Graber was our hero of the day. He drove the potholed road returning us to town at record speed.

Another miracle happened when the airline agents issued the tickets in a record fifteen minutes. Archie repeated his axle cracking drive back to the airport. I'm sure we hit the roof of the vehicle a dozen times or more.

The plane had just arrived, an hour late, but *right on time for us!* The MBMS missionaries had reserved eight places. We purchased nine tickets. That was the first part of our miracle. The extra ticket was *mine.* I was hoping somehow to get on that aircraft. Because of the national crisis, Air Congo was *booked solid* from Kikwit to Kinshasa for weeks to come. If I hadn't been able to get on this flight, I would have once again been stranded in the interior for an indefinite period.

In the rush of boarding the aircraft, the agent didn't

bother to count our group, but just took the wad of tickets in hand and waved us on. That was the second part of our miracle. We hastily boarded. The young Nickel boys sat on our laps, traded back and forth during the two-hour flight to Kinshasa. I could hardly believe it when the plane touched down.

What amazing and inconceivable answers to our prayers. To *my* prayers. I had new appreciation for those who spoke of "living by faith" and for what the concept of "deliverance" meant, up-close and personal. I really felt convinced that God had provided for me. How else could I have explained all of the things that had happened?

I wrote the following conclusion in a letter to Betty Jean sent on the *same day I arrived back in Kinshasa*, July 26, 1967:

"As I look back now on the last six weeks or so in Pai Kongila I am really thankful for the experience. I have most certainly grown closer to God, learned to confide more in Him and to trust in a way I perhaps never had to do before. In a way I'm really glad He didn't listen to some of my shortsighted requests but showed me His plan, a better one, instead. Some of the experiences I had during the extended part of my stay I wouldn't trade for anything; God must sometimes work that way. When we finally come to the place where we humble ourselves and admit that it's got to

be His affair, that we don't have the answers, then He provides them. In response to my searching I found this Scripture that really spoke to me: "So humble yourselves under God's hand and in His own good time He will lift you up. You can throw the whole weight of your anxieties upon Him for you are His personal concern." (I Peter 5:6, 7 Phillips)

Postscript: An additional word of perspective is appropriate here. The efforts of North American missionaries like the Nickels, Voths, and Penners and Congolese pastors and church leaders like Bernard Kasai have had a truly impressive impact over time. There are now approximately 100,000 Mennonite Brethren Christians in Congo, principally in Bandundu Province – which includes Pai Kongila – and in Kinshasa. That total compares to about 70,000 MBs in the U.S., Canada, and Mexico combined.

35
The Emergence of the MPR

"If you would understand anything, observe its beginning and its development."
— Aristotle

T he end of the summer of 1967 marked *year one* of our sojourn in Africa. What an eventful year it had been for the two of us Oregon boys! We had certainly been stretched far outside of our comfort zones in nearly every area of our lives: physically, emotionally, spiritually and socially.

By our second August in the Congo we had made it, more or less successfully, through the most disabling aspects of culture shock and had actually begun to move about Kinshasa in a more confident manner. Knowing a few words of French and Lingala helped. What might have helped even more would have been a stable social and political context, but that was simply not the Congo of the 1960s. Perhaps a bit more background information would be helpful at this point in my descriptions since Jim and I were about to encounter Congo politics up close and personal.

The Congo traces its modern history to the late 1870s when, following the exploration of Sir Henry Morton Stanley under the sponsorship of King Leopold II of Belgium, the administration of the country came under the latter's royal auspices. In fact, King Leopold named the huge region "The Congo Free State" and made the land his private property. It occurs to me that perhaps Leopold's real meaning in the naming of his private reserve was *"free to take whatever I want."* The capitol was named after the King: Leopoldville. His was not a benevolent rule, as one might surmise from this huge land grab. The population was systematically brutalized so that the King's agents could extract large rubber and ivory quotas. Some historians speculate that nearly half the population died during this period. Leopold, however, become extremely wealthy. Famous writers of the era such as Mark Twain and Arthur Conan Doyle protested the grimly exploitive administration of the people and land. Joseph Conrad's *Heart of Darkness* was written about this "far-from-free state."

In 1908, bowing to international pressure, the Belgian parliament reluctantly took over the colonial administration and the land became officially known as *the Belgian Congo* for the next half century. Unfortunately, the harsh and autocratic legacy of King Leopold's regime continued in the colonial administration of the Belgian Congo.

Following international pressure and in response to a series of riots and demands for independent nation status in the Congo during the 1950s, the Belgian government declared The Republic of Congo to be independent on June 30, 1960. The country was ill prepared for this move, however. There were few educated Congolese at independence; some say only thirteen college graduates in total. The new country possessed virtually no political experience or consensus in a culture historically dominated by geographic, tribal and cultural divides.

It didn't take long for the Congo to slide into chaos as the military mutinied against their white Belgian officers. Armed soldiers and scores of unemployed youth filled the streets of the main cities, rioting and recriminating against former oppressors and resident Europeans.

Congo politics in the first four years of independence was characterized by a series of confusing and alarming power struggles as first one set of leaders and then another attempted to consolidate the central government's power. There were betrayals, assassinations and a series of secession movements by the largest and most mineral-rich regions of the country: Katanga, the South Kasai and Oriental provinces. UN troops were summoned and deployed to bring order, but their intervention was controversial and added to the violence and turmoil of the fledgling nation. The Soviet Union, Belgium and the US all participated in efforts to quell the various secession movements.

In 1964 a violent "Simba" revolt took place in the Kisangani, Stanleyville, region. It gained the attention of the international community when the rebels, fearing defeat, took over 1,800 Europeans hostage. The combined efforts of Belgian and US military finally freed the hostages in a dramatic rescue and quelled the revolt.

By November, 1965, the head of the army, General Joseph Mobutu, seized power in a coup supported by Western interests, notably the CIA. Mobutu established a single-party state and killed, imprisoned or expelled his opposition. Though firmly in power in Kinshasa, Mobutu's regime continued to be threatened by two mercenary-led mutinies in the mineral-rich Katanga Provence. The first took place in 1966 and was short lived.

The second so-called *Kisangani Mutiny* emerged in the summer of 1967, the time covered in the previous "Pai Kongila" chapters of this story and continued into the events to be described in the next chapters of this memoir. A Belgian settler by the name of Jean Schramme led this rebellion. He along with about 1,100 Katangese troops held off the 32,000-man Congolese National Army from July until November of 1967. At that point they safely escaped into Rwanda and the Congo finally settled into a semblance of political stability.

About this same time, late summer 1967, the Popular Movement of the Revolution (French: *Mouvement*

Populaire de la Revolution or MPR) party was established by Mobutu largely as a means of prompting popular support for his threatened regime. Its ideology centered on the notion of nationalism and "authenticity." All citizens from birth were compulsory members of the party and as such, encouraged to adopt and utilize only native, non-Western names, to wear African-style clothing and to unquestioningly support the initiatives of their leader, Mobutu.

Mobutu insisted that it was authentically African to have only one leader and one party, not several. By 1966 Mobutu renamed the country's principal cities: Leopoldville to Kinshasa, Stanleyville to Kisangani, a move designed to strengthen national identity. He later changed the name of the country to Zaire and his own name to Mobutu *Sese Seko*, referring to himself as the Father of the Country, "the Guide" and the embodiment of the MPR. No problem with lack of ego there!

Mobutu wanted there to be *no doubt* who was in charge of the country and what was expected of the populace: strong and enthusiastic support.

The above sketch had special meaning for Westerners residing in Kinshasa in August of 1967 such as my TASOK colleagues and me. We were regularly reminded that we were outsiders living in an era of considerable political turmoil. Much of the Congo's recent history had been violent and some of that pent up hostility was, perhaps appropriately, directed toward expatriates.

It didn't feel very safe.

The new President Mobutu was obsessed with control. One manifestation of that single-minded focus was the presence of military roadblocks wherever we drove. The fact that white mercenaries had been so active in the recent history of the country made us as young white males, immediately *suspect* at these stops. In those days we noticed lots of signs of the MPR: posters, road signs, and clothing all bore the face of Mobutu and colors of the party. The MPR was an obvious instrument of the government's effort to build a strong power base. Our encounter with this party became up-close and personal.

36

A Political Arrival

"It is only in adventure that some people succeed in knowing themselves."

– André Gide

T he announcement of a national MPR rally day on the very date we expected the arrival of four new Christian Service TASOK teachers caught us by surprise. What could that mean? We didn't fully grasp what such an event might entail. The purpose of a political rally day in 1960s Congo, carried very different meanings from anything we had ever understood a political rally to be about in the U.S. None of this was clear to us at the time. Since the MPR was a new phenomenon, apparently many of the veteran missionaries did not know what to expect either.

At about 5 AM on a cool, 65-degree pre-dawn morning we found ourselves heading toward the Ndjili Airport to welcome our peers who were scheduled to arrive on the 6 AM Sabena Airlines flight from Brussels. Others would transport them and their things, but Jim and I didn't want to miss being on hand to welcome them personally. Our greeter-less arrival in the Congo the previous summer motivated this pre-dawn excursion.

The passage through the dark streets for the first half of the 13-mile drive to the airport was uneventful. There were streetlights on the main boulevards, but only the ones in the downtown area were regularly maintained so much of the drive was in darkness. The police were not typically out before dawn so our alert status was several notches lower than usual.

We were more than halfway to our destination when we came upon a group of cars stopped in front of some barriers consisting of oil drums and boards. There was a small crowd standing in front of a dozen or more stopped vehicles. We recognized several of the senior missionaries and other familiar American faces in the group. They were standing in a semi-circle speaking very intently with the apparent leaders of an even larger group of Congolese.

Most of the nationals wore bright MPR kerchiefs. These were the colors of the party and this was a national political rally day. The tone of the French and Kituba exchanges appeared angry and frustrated: angry on the part of the Congolese, and frustrated on the part of the Americans.

We exited our little two-door Fiat 600 car and asked

one of the missionaries what was happening. He explained that an MPR rally had been called to protest Belgian support of the mercenaries who were assisting in the rebellion taking place in Katanga province. The rally leaders indicated that they suspected more mercenaries could be arriving on the Belgian Sabena flight. As a result, all traffic to the airport was being halted.

"Whaaaat?" was our response.

"How are the new teachers supposed to get to their new home?"

We were anxious to meet them and at the time we simply did not think the roadblock was something to take seriously.

I motioned to two of the Congolese sporting bright, new MPR kerchiefs and pointed up the road, "A l'aeroport?" I said in my best pidgin French. They both nodded vigorously and crawled in the back seat of our small car. They waved at their buddies as Jim simply drove, unchallenged, around the barriers. We felt pretty smart that as Congo novices we were getting past the roadblock while the veterans were all being delayed.

As I look back over the years, I'm not sure what motivated Jim and me to head out when everyone else was detained. It was an impulsive action. An adventure. The kind of thing one might expect of 23-year-olds who don't have enough experience or good sense to recognize trouble.

A mile or two up the very empty road we came

to a second roadblock. This barrier was similar to the previous one except there were fewer cars stopped. As we approached the roadway obstacles, one of our Congolese passengers took off his MPR kerchief and waved it out the window. We were hand-motioned on around the barrier and continued on our way. What a relief!

We hadn't proceeded very far, however, when we came to a third roadblock. Here, we stopped and our MPR passengers briefly exited the car, engaging in some discussion with those at the barriers before piling back in.

"OK?" I quizzed. "Ça va" was their reply.

As we continued along the completely deserted road it was beginning to dawn on Jim and me that we were *way out there*, away from help and only marginally able to communicate.

"I sure hope we're done with the roadblocks," I quietly murmured to him.

Unfortunately, we weren't.

As we came over a slight rise in the road, a large agitated crowd filled the street. There were cement blocks and boards blocking the roadway. The noise was loud and chaotic. Portable radios were blaring "Congo jazz" with its singsong patterns and steel guitar trills. As we pulled up people were yelling and those who ran up to our car appeared wild-eyed and excited. Our two MPR escorts motioned to be let out and they promptly disappeared into the crowd.

Not a good sign.

I stepped out of the car to speak to the leader, or at least the person I assumed was in charge. He was an angry looking Congolese wearing a Mobutu-style hat in addition to the usual MPR kerchief. He stood, scowling with his arms folded. People surrounded our car. Two or three fellows behind the vehicle were attempting to push it off the road as others tried to grab for the keys through Jim's open window. I yelled at him to put the keys in his pocket, which he did. I hooked my left arm through the open window frame, dug my heels in and pulled back to counter the efforts being made to move our Fiat, as the leader addressed me.

"Bino - bokay wapi?" You, where are you going? he demanded in Lingala.

What happened then I would later recount as the single time in my entire life that I lay claim to have *"spoken in tongues."* By that, I mean that I started jabbering in a combination of Lingala and French and I believe the other party comprehended it. It was inspired speech.

I indicated to the MPR leader that we were Protestant missionary teachers and that we had heard there was big danger at the airport where our friends who were also Protestant missionaries, had just arrived. We wanted to get there and make sure they were safe.

Well, that's what I *intended* to say, anyhow.

Perhaps only God knows what I *actually* said, but whatever it was, after a pause, the pushing, yelling, music and chaos continuing around us, the stern leader pointed his finger at me and said, *"Kenda!"* but I understood him to also say "don't return before 5 PM or there will be big trouble – *Likambo monene!"* He then yelled something to the men pushing our car and they quickly stood up and backed off. He was exercising his authority. Cement blocks were moved. Jim started the car and drove us through the barrier.

In speculating about the MPR leader's actions later, we wondered if he let us go because I had identified ourselves as Protestant missionaries. Perhaps, unlike Catholic expatriates, we were not identified as closely with the hated colonial establishment. Or, was releasing us just an opportunity for the headman to exercise and demonstrate his authority to his followers? On a spiritual tone, was this an instance of some sort of Divine deliverance? Was it *all of the above?*

Whatever the reason for our release, we were hugely relieved to have the mob and noise behind us at last.

"Now what?" we thought.

Things had escalated further than my comfort zone limits after the *first* roadblock. Would there be military roadblocks next? Would the army be surrounding the airport? Is it possible mercenaries actually *were* on the flight? Would there be shooting? Since we couldn't turn back what *would* we do?

I burst out in a full sweat. I noticed that the car was weaving because Jim's hands on the steering wheel were shaking. He briefly pulled over and we discussed the above worries, concluding finally that we had no real choice but to continue on and just see what would happen.

We said a brief prayer, something like "God - help us, we don't know what we've gotten ourselves into" and continued on the eerily deserted road to Ndjili Airport.

As the airport facility came into sight our first reaction was *relief.* All was quiet. Nothing was moving. No military vehicles, no Congolese walking by the road, no cars coming or going. Happily, no sounds of gunfire.

Quiet.

We saw the Sabena aircraft on the tarmac behind the terminal, so we knew the flight had arrived. We drove into the parking lot and walked into the building. Throughout the main lobby, there were small clutches of people from the flight scattered in groups with their luggage.

Jim first noticed a young man at the Sabena desk speaking with one of the agents. He looked both tired and scared. That *had* to be Dave Klaassen, one of our party of four new teachers! He had safely arrived with his wife, Ruth, and two other single teachers, Amy Dahl and Elaine Bonnet. Jim approached him and introduced himself as I followed close behind.

I'll pick up the story at this point with Dave Klaassen's report of that encounter. This is an excerpt from his first letter home written to his parents and shared with me as I researched this event:

"The plane landed at 5:30 am instead of 6:00 am so we weren't surprised when there was no one there. Amazingly we had no trouble getting through customs. They never even looked at our health certificates. It was a little disillusioning to go into the immigration office and find the Congolese official (a young military enlistee) sound asleep with Superman comic books all over his desk.

Then we went to pick up our luggage that they never opened. All I paid was 1000 francs (about $2.00) to get the camera through. At least I guess that's what it was for. The guy said "moh-NAY" so I gave him some. Oh, well.

By this time it was 6:15 am and no one was there so we began to wonder. No one spoke English so we had no way of knowing what was wrong. I went to the Sabena desk to call the M.B. Mission (Ed. Note: Mennonite Brethren Mission) and the man, would you believe someone who finally spoke English, said there were roadblocks and no one could get to the airport.

About then I might have started to worry but Jim Becker tapped me on the shoulder. He and John Franz had talked their way through 4 roadblocks and had the scare of their lives. George Faul and Fred Epp (Ed. Note: senior missionaries) were turned back. The result was that we all sat in the airport until 3:00 p.m. when we figured the troops would be gone, which they were. These were not the army. They were a sort of youth corps known as the MPR. I don't understand the whole thing, but apparently they were called out by Mobutu as a show of strength against a reputed band of mercenaries who were supposed to be on our plane.

Meanwhile, downtown a group was breaking all the windows on one side of the main street and setting fire to the Belgian embassy."

Jim and I had a good portion of the day to get acquainted with our newly arrived Christian Service colleagues, since *nothing* was moving on the airport road. We regaled our new teammates with the story of our morning's adventure. I'm sure we repeated it several times. It all seemed so remarkable to us. We had been the last vehicle to make it through the roadblocks that day. We were more amazed we made it and grateful to be in one piece, than proud of our accomplishment. It was clear to us then as it is now that far more naiveté than courage was at play.

In the subsequent unfolding of events, a series of phone calls was made from the airport to the U. S. Embassy and by late afternoon a small convoy of four military jeeps arrived. One had the official flag of the U. S. Embassy. Menno Travel followed this convoy with their kombi. We were the last of just a very few cars to have gotten through to the airport that morning.

We loaded our colleagues and their luggage into the kombi and caravanned back through the city to the

TASOK compound. Others were eagerly awaiting our arrival. On the drive through Kinshasa we noticed several burned out vehicles that were still smoldering by the side of the road. In the days that followed we heard of other incidents of violence and vandalism that punctuated the day. We were fortunate fellows.

I'm quite sure that we failed to understand or appreciate the history that was taking place at the time of the above events. As we learned more about Congo's checkered past our insight into the obstructive behavior we encountered deepened: roadblocks, power assertion, resentment of whites, and demands of local officials.

Conversely, we came to appreciate the patience, endurance and tenacity of average Congolese. For most of them daily life, employment, food, transport, and health, was infinitely more challenging than were the inconveniences we experienced as whites living in their land.

37

Settling in to a Second Year

"The happiest people are those too busy to know whether they are or not"
– William Feather

My second year of teaching at the American School of Kinshasa presented its own set of busy routines. There were daily class preparations to make for biology and junior high science classes. My subject matter utilized labs and with an absence of materials and planning resources it took a good deal of creativity and time for me to figure out what in the world I was going to teach and how I would present it.

Jim and I met weekly with a small group of high school boys for a combination Bible study and bull session. Those were both interesting and challenging encounters. The fearless fellows asked us questions about things we had never even thought about previously. Are there animals in heaven? When do pre-born babies acquire a soul? What do people do after they die? If multiple marriage is forbidden, how do you explain the Old Testament practices?

I served as the sponsor of the church's high school youth group and was also the junior class sponsor at school. These responsibilities necessitated attendance at regular meetings and events and provided new insights into the lives of my students. Most were impressively able and motivated learners.

I acted as TASOK's student council advisor and the letterman's club advisor and as such became the liaison with the school administration for their various projects and issues. As the appointed head of the athletic department for TASOK, I ordered equipment, catalogued items, developed curriculum and devised schedules for intermural and school sports.

John & Dave K. time runners in P.E. class

In sum, I was busy and engaged in a variety of second-year work assignments.

In my second year as basketball coach I was finally able to schedule several games against Congolese secondary-school opponents. Up to that point our opponents had consisted of ad hoc groups of American missionaries, TASOK teachers, volunteer workers, U.S. Embassy military attachés and so on. All of our opponents were familiar with U. S. basketball rules and play. Facing age-peer Congolese opponents was quite a cross-cultural experience for both my basketball players and for me as their coach.

As a former basketball letterman on a Division I West Coast U.S. team, I thought that I knew the sport very well. I did. However, not the kind played in the Congo! International basketball rules were permissive; play was wide open, full-blast with an aggressive, cast-off-shooting and cross-court-passing style that left us all wondering whether we were even playing the same sport as our opposition. Our young African opponents delightedly *slaughtered us* until we finally started figuring out this new system.

Leisure routines in the Congo during the mid-60s developed a certain predictability of their own. I've already described afternoon siesta-hour swims that single teachers and students enjoyed each week in an Olympic-sized swimming pool not far from the school. Our visits to the pool were less frequent in my second year. That was mostly a function of being busier in the afternoons, with added work duties. Perhaps, for me it was also a matter of having less incentive to go – Betty Jean was not there!

TASOK Condors with coach Franz (back right)

Thursday nights for most of the first year and into the second, were set aside for competition. Sometimes it was the single guys vs. the local married missionaries; other times it was a recruited group of available players willing to take on local teams, a Greek team, the Funa Athletic Club, Belgians and other groups we discovered in rousing volleyball and basketball matches under the lights of the American School.

Competition was intense and sometimes brutal. Pacifist ideology appeared to be fully suspended for these matches. I remember wondering if a couple of the resident Mennonite missionaries didn't have serious anger management issues: when their attempts to score were effectively blocked they actively retaliated! These evenings usually concluded on a positive note, however, with the entire pack of sweaty ball players drinking cold sodas at the residence of one of the missionaries. Post-competition interaction was punctuated with lots of good-natured kidding and laugh-out-loud humor. In retrospect, these evenings of competition probably also served as a good test of our spirituality.

Weekly excursions to the market, the bakery and to various social events such as Friday movies in English at a U. S. Embassy residence, also assumed a predictable pattern by the fall of 1967. Jim and I shared the use of a tiny Fiat 600 two-door car and we also were assigned two robin's-egg-blue Vespa scooters. We rarely used these to travel any distance across town or after dark since traffic could be treacherous. Helmets? Never heard of them at the time.

One repeated transportation experience we could have lived without in those days was the surprise stops we were subject to whenever we returned to our apartments after dark. Our residences were in the school compound located on a side road parallel to a main highway. Just across the main road was a large army camp surrounding President Mobutu's palace. Large trees and jungle-like foliage lined the dirt road that ran past the school and there were no other dwellings on that road. It was dark and frankly kind of spooky to turn off the main road and head for the gate leading to our apartments.

Our evening adrenaline rush came in the following manner. As we approached the darkest section of the road, suddenly out from the trees would spring several armed men dressed in military fatigues. We would be ordered out of our car, it would be "searched", supposedly for weapons and our papers would be checked. We would then be quizzed in Congo-French or Lingala. Why were we there? Who were we? What were we doing so close to the army base? And so on.

Our communication skills were pretty marginal but this was a regular routine we were subjected to until the Katanga rebellion was finally resolved in November. The same soldiers performed this little psychodrama each time and they knew full well who we were after several stops. That didn't prevent them from enjoying the opportunity to hassle us. Perhaps they hoped to one-day find something worth confiscating in our vehicle.

Even though these regular "rousting's" could be anticipated, we still found it pretty unsettling to have armed men stop us at gunpoint in the dark and put us through their hassles. I suppose in retrospect we could have purchased some peace of mind, *cheap*, had we offered the soldiers a few francs. We were too frugal, naive and idealistic to even consider that strategy.

Sunday mornings we attended services at the Kalina English-speaking Protestant church. In those days there were as many as 500 or more people in attendance on any given Sunday morning. The church, originally constructed in 1915, was located on the British Baptist grounds and followed traditions of that original sponsoring group. The thick hymnals had no music symbols, just hymn titles and verses, verses, verses.

Sunday morning services at Kalina were liturgical, comprised of responsive Scripture reading leading to long sermons read from an elevated podium in the front corner of the church. The singing of ponderously slow hymns that had at least six verses followed these messages. We sang them all.

This was certainly a different worship tradition than I was used to. Sunday morning church was, however, one of the key gathering points of the greater English-speaking expatriate community, so it was an excellent venue for seeing who might have entered the country during a given week. Attendees included not only missionaries but also business, embassy and military attachés. There were always interesting people coming and going.

Kalina Protestant church on busy Sunday morning

Sunday evenings were, to me, a welcome contrast to the stoic events of the morning. The missionary community regularly gathered in the late afternoon at the historic Sims Chapel, a modest structure built by pioneer Dr. Aaron Sims in 1891 near the American Baptist mission compound. We joined these events in the on-again-off-again fashion that characterizes young adult participation in church activities.

The early part of the evening consisted of a pot-luck picnic on the side of the hill overlooking Stanley Pool and the Congo River. Then, the remainder of the evening was filled with an informal worship service. It typically consisted of enthusiastic singing of familiar choruses and up-beat Christian songs and special music such as duets, quartets or instrumental solos. A devotional message followed, typically short, practical and to the point. I remember them as positive, enjoyable evenings that were far more attuned to my expectations of worship than the Sunday morning services.

These snapshots provide a composite picture of life in the second year of my Congo service. Life unfolded in a series of routines, but of course this was Africa and there are always exceptions.

38

It's a Steal!

"The rate at which a person can mature is directly proportional to the embarrassment he can endure."
– Douglas Engelbart

O ne of the exceptions to my routines came about in an unusual manner. Wednesday nights were a time reserved for Bible study and prayer among Mennonite Brethren expatriates living in Kinshasa. As M. B. Christian Service volunteers, Jim and I felt some pressure to attend these small group sessions. The pressure came in subtle questions by regular attendees about what we were doing on Wednesday evenings and via statements by some of the resident missionaries such as, "we'd love to have you join us," or "please consider making it a priority," or "your presence would be a real encouragement to us." That sort of thing.

We attended the Bible study and prayer sessions on a sporadic basis. We found we were typically the youngest attendees by at least 15 or more years and we perceived the level of dialogue to be rather superficial and predictable. This pejorative assessment certainly isn't meant as a final definition or judgment as to the value of those gatherings. They appeared to be meaningful to some people. However, as 23-year-olds we felt constrained by the traditionalism of the evenings and looked for excuses to miss attending.

One missed M. B. Bible study evening stands out in my memory. I believe Jim and I had confirmed with one of the regulars that we would be in attendance on a particular Wednesday night. On the way to the Bible study, however, we changed our minds. There was an outdoor movie – chairs, not a drive-in – showing in a theater several kilometers from the meeting. The movie title was *"Un Homme et Une Femme,"* a French film released in 1966. The title sounded racy enough for two hormone-filled young men so we decided on a whim to go *there* rather than to Bible study. This was a decision we would shortly regret.

Jim pulled our grey Fiat 600 into a parking space directly in front of the entry door to the theater. An elderly Congolese man sat on a rickety chair to one side of the door. He had a machete on his lap and we recognized him as the theater's guard.

"Good," I thought "we won't have to shell out to street urchins to "guard" our car," i.e. pay one of them so they wouldn't remove our rear view mirrors or tail light covers.

The film itself was a huge disappointment. First, our comprehension of French was minimal. I doubt we recognized more than a handful of words. Then, the action was tame, consisting of long dialogues with frequent flashback segues of full color, black-and-white and sepia-toned images.

What a boring evening. After an hour and forty-some *long* minutes of exposure to this disappointing non-entertainment we exited the venue.

We headed out the doorway toward our – "Hey! Where's our car?"

It was gone.

As we stood there, mouths gaping, other theater patrons, mostly white Europeans, quickly entered their vehicles and drove away, one after another. The elderly theater guard was still in his chair.

"Whapi voiture na biso?" – Where's our car? I demanded in my best pidgin-Lingala.

"Nini?" – What? Was his eloquent reply.

I repeated my query and he shrugged he didn't know. When I pressed him, limited vocabulary that I had, he said something about two "citizens" – Mobutuism for Congolese nationals – having taken it. He then just pointed down the street.

It was likely that the car thieves either paid off or threatened the guard. In his defense, I'd guess the old fellow would have taken the worse end of *any* serious attempt to intervene in a theft.

I then proceeded to yell the French word for thief,

"*voleur*", as loudly as I could, but by that time the only people near enough to hear me were a European couple heading for their car. They just shook their heads and lifted their hands in futility. With that grand elucidation I'd just used up my entire repertoire of coping strategies for our present crisis. Now what?

This event took place long before the age of cell phones. There were no phone booths in Kinshasa, Congo, even if we had had a number to dial. We started walking. It was several kilometers down a dimly lit main boulevard to a side street leading to the TASOK teacher's compound where we could get a ride back up the hill to our apartments. Night was not an advisable time for young white men to be out on foot in the big city. We were sitting, well, *walking* ducks.

After about 25 minutes of hoofing it without incident a car slowed and the driver rolled down his window. It was one of the TASOK elementary teachers returning from some social event. He graciously dropped us off at the teachers' compound. We reported the theft of our vehicle to the grade school principal who lived there and were then delivered to our apartments up the hill near the new school.

The next day, accompanied by TASOK's treasurer, Jerry Weaver, we drove to the police station and with his help, made a stolen vehicle report. This was no simple matter. It involved working with a Congolese police officer who tediously prepared a several page report, making four or five carbon paper copies of each page, using hunt-and-peck, single-finger typing. The clerk made numerous mistakes that had to be "erased" from each copy and at least one time he wadded up a whole page with copies, discarded them and started over.

We were there for *hours*. Perhaps the poor fellow had nothing better to do that day. Maybe he was somehow hoping that his pace would motivate extra revenue from the complainants. The man could have just been incompetent. Whatever the source of this snail-paced bureaucrat's work style, we finally obtained the official police report that our insurance company required.

For several months after our car disappeared, someone from the school called each week to the police station to see if by any chance our little Fiat had been recovered. Each time they were told that there was no word, and that they'd call if anything came up.

Finally, we just stopped checking.

It wasn't more than three weeks later that a call indeed did come to the TASOK office one morning. It was from the police station in the Kinshasa precinct where our car had been taken. They had our car. Would we please come and pick it up?

When the school officials inquired further they found out that the stolen car had been recovered on the *same day it was taken* but that the police had been "unable to reach the owners" and so they had used it themselves. The Fiat was now, unfortunately, no longer running, as the engine had been blown from lack of oil.

John with Fiat that later disappeared

Oh yes, the final straw. The police informed us that when they recovered the vehicle *"the tires were missing."* The reporting officer had generously supplied tires from a relative who coincidently happened to have some of the correct size. We could therefore either purchase these tires for a good price when we collected our vehicle, or the officer would keep them and we could buy our own.

Of course, in reality the hubcaps were still dusty and intact and those were certainly our car's original tires. Such a proposition illustrated the joys and justice of routine contacts with public safety in the Congo.

Postscript: You've probably already guessed the reaction we received from more than one of our Bible study group members when the word got out about our vehicle being stolen on the very night the faithful were meeting. The fact that Jim and I were attending a movie when it happened – such entertainment options were off limits for some of the attendees – only caused eyebrows to arch even higher.

On our part, we had to wonder if God doesn't have a sense of humor, after all. He at least has a keen sense of irony!

39

South African Holiday

=====((O))=====

"Surprise is the greatest gift which life can grant us."
– Boris Pasternak

A s 1967 drew to a close, the events in the U.S. and around the world reminded us that we were living in tumultuous times. Voice of America news reports as well as Newsweek's international edition kept us appraised of current events in our home country and abroad. The U.S. troop build-up in Viet Nam had exceeded half a million, more than the Korean War at its peak. Antiwar protests were increasing including a huge march on the Pentagon in October. Israel defeated Arab forces in the historic and controversial "Six-day War," occupying the Sinai Peninsula and other territories. Thurgood Marshall became the first black U.S. Supreme Court Justice amid nation-wide racial turmoil. The so-called "summer of love" ended with violent race riots in Detroit, Newark and 125 other cities, destroying over 1,700 businesses, killing 43 people and injuring hundreds of others. The level of discontent with government in general and toward war and social justice issues in particular was at an all-time high.

Like a rock in a pond, the ripple effect of these historic events eventually reached us on the continent of Africa. One effect was to heighten our awareness as Americans living abroad that we were not especially popular world citizens. This was a new revelation for us. Our government's policies became a source of inquiry and challenge whenever we encountered English-speaking foreigners. I recall these exchanges as awkward and embarrassing experiences. I did not agree with many of the official positions of my government, finding them hard to explain and impossible to defend.

Another impact of 1967's newsworthy events was to limit where we could travel. As other young Americans living and working abroad attempted to export their U.S. fueled social justice activism and idealism, host governments were offended. Expulsions and travel restrictions were imposed as a consequence. According to Stanley Meisler's 2011 book on the Peace Corps, *When the World Calls: The inside story of the Peace Corps and its first 50 years*, exported activism was a major issue for volunteers serving in the Corps during the mid 60s.

Nowhere was this of greater concern than to the Apartheid regime of South Africa. Peace Corps volunteers serving in near-by countries were not welcome to visit 1967 South Africa. The Peace Corps itself did not officially enter the country until thirty years later in post-Apartheid 1997.

Well aware of the above circumstances, it therefore came as a genuine surprise to Jim and me when we received a phone call from Menno Travel in downtown Kinshasa just a few days before Christmas that our visas to visit South Africa had been *approved*. We had actually hoped to complete our aborted summer plans to visit East Africa during our Christmas break and had only applied for the South Africa visas as a back-up, albeit, a remote one. However, after two disappointing trips to the Ndjili Airport to board an Air Congo flight to Goma in the east, we had finally given up on taking our Christmas vacation outside of the country.

On our first trip to the airport we discovered that our scheduled flight had been inexplicably cancelled. We were told only five of the Air Congo fleet of 22 planes were flying after locals took over the maintenance of the aircrafts. We quickly booked seats for the next day's flight. Our second airport run was vintage 1960s Congo as well: reportedly, an army General and his entourage had shown up and commandeered the aircraft to take them to their chosen destination. The plane had already departed an hour before we showed up to claim our reserved seats.

Discouraged, we returned to our apartment. Jim and I decided to pray about this matter, expressing to God that if He wanted to allow us to have a vacation

He would have to do something about it. We were just plain out of ideas as to what more *we* could do to make it happen. The phone call we received the very next morning was thus more than just a surprise; we viewed it as an answer to prayer.

"The next flight to Johannesburg is tomorrow. It's a once-a-week flight. So, do you want to take the visas and go, or not?" was the pointed query of Menno Travel clerk Anita Penner. Jim and I looked at each other. No problem deciding this one!

"We'll take them," was our reply in unison.

We joyfully returned to our apartment from the TASOK office where we had received the call and hastily packed our bags. What an unexpected opportunity! We then drove to the Menno Travel office to retrieve our visas and purchase our plane tickets.

"What should we do in South Africa?" we asked Anita upon our arrival at her office.

She pulled some brochures from her files and we glanced over them. Many of the spots depicted were exotic: game parks, beaches, diamond mines, and so on. Others were at a considerable distance from Johannesburg, our flight destination. All were more expensive than we could afford.

"I guess we'll just hang out for two weeks in Jo'burg," I said as Jim nodded in resigned agreement.

As we were preparing to leave, Anita paused and thoughtfully mused: "You know, I have a cousin from home in Abbotsford, BC, who is a TEAM missionary in

Durban. Here's her name and number, just in case you happen to find your way there."

Anita's casual afterthought proved to be a significant key to our subsequent South African adventures. After picking up some additional information about Johannesburg we left the office.

The next morning we boarded our plane in Kinshasa and flew to South Africa.

During the four-hour KLM Airlines flight to Johannesburg Jim and I celebrated our good fortune in being able to leave our assignment and travel to an English-speaking locale for our holiday. I remember being pretty excited about getting on a big plane and going somewhere once again after a year and a half of being "in country." It was good to get away, *anywhere*.

During our flight we looked over the brochures from the travel agency and concluded that we would likely have to settle for asking the concierge at our hotel what suggestions he might have for entertaining ourselves during our South Africa stay. We had little money and few ideas. Our provisional plan was to go to a few English-language movies and find some good places to eat.

We arrived in Johannesburg and spent some time at the airport calling around for available rooms. We took the first hotel that had space. Jim and I then boarded the airport bus, traveled to a central stop in the downtown area and walked the short distance to our hotel. The first thing we did after getting settled in our room was to locate a nearby market and purchase watermelon, peaches, grapes, 7-up and a variety of other "goodies" that were unavailable in the Congo. How good it was. I remember thinking, "These delicacies will *never* taste this good again." I was right.

We spent the next day discovering more special things to eat, doing some sightseeing in the city and moving to a different hotel. We considered our first hotel to be a bit over budget at $5/night, so we located a less "expensive" room and made the switch. We also went to a movie that evening. It was a new release entitled *"The Valley of the Dolls."* We had read about the movie in Newsweek and it seemed like it would be an entertainment morsel to savor. On that point we bombed royally.

Valley of the Dolls was a popular drama universally panned by critics, but one that topped the charts in box office revenue. It was based on Jacqueline Suzanne's 1966 novel about "dolls," slang for "downers", mood-altering drugs. What a dumb story line and over-the-top acting! One of the starring actresses, Lee Grant, said in a later interview that she considered it the "best and funniest worst movie ever made!" Co-star Barbara Perkins echoed her sentiments, telling a sold out crowd at a 1997 screening: "I know why you like it; because it's *so bad!*"

Yep. That was our first English-speaking movie in South Africa. I think we chuckled through the second half of the movie as first one and then another of the key characters met disaster after disaster from their lack of simple judgment and incredibly bad choices. Memorable.

The other memorable thing that marked our entry to South African society was the policy of Apartheid. Neither Jim nor I were particularly well read in history or political science so we had only vague images of what this infamous culture might be like. We were therefore startled to come across drinking fountains and restrooms that bore "Whites only" signs.

The people of color we observed on the busy Johannesburg streets were dressed a good deal more prosperously than were those we were accustomed to seeing in Kinshasa. However, non-whites including Asians, Indians and persons of mixed race as well as blacks, clearly kept their distance from whites. It was only other white persons who made eye contact with us as we passed them on the street. In the evenings the city streets were nearly deserted. With few exceptions, those who moved about freely after dark were all Caucasians.

While we felt reasonably safe as white males, we openly wondered what life must be like for those who didn't share the privilege of our skin color. It was all very disconcerting for us as idealistic young men. Even then, the prosperity we observed clearly came at too high a price for the majority of the country's citizenry, or so we concluded.

40

An Apartheid Christmas

"There are no strangers on Christmas Eve."
– Mildred Cram and Adele Comandini

The key question for us was what to do during our sojourn in South Africa. We had arrived with very meager resources and even less knowledge of our options.

We inquired of various people we met in our first two days in Johannesburg what they might recommend that we see or do during our brief stay in their country. Several individuals mentioned that we might especially enjoy visiting Durban, a resort town on the Indian Ocean. It was a particularly popular destination spot for South Africans at Christmas time.

The only problem with this suggestion was its 365-mile distance from our Johannesburg location. That and our lack of transportation. "No problem" we were told. Young South African men, typically in the military, taped onto the side of their bags the initials of the province they wished to visit. They then stood by the highway and people would willingly pick them up, a unique version of hitchhiking. We decided to give it a try. It was Christmas Eve day.

More than four decades later, as I reflect on our decision to hitchhike over three hundred miles in a strange land to an unfamiliar place, I wonder how in the world we ever thought it was a good idea, let alone a reasonable course of action. I suppose the answer lay somewhere between our being naïve and adventurous. Perhaps we received enough reassurance from friendly South Africans at the time that it seemed like something we should do. We had no idea where we'd stay or exactly what we'd do when and if we made it to Durban.

We prayed, committing our journey to God for guidance. That seemed like an appropriate thing to do at the time. Then, we followed the instructions we had been given. We taped "ZN" on our bags, for KwaZulu-Natal Province, and headed for the highway leading in a southeast direction.

Adventure.

We did not have to wait long for a ride. A lady and her young daughter were the first to offer us a lift. Thinking about it now, that seems to me like a pretty unwise thing for her to have done; how could she know what kind of characters she had just picked up? As I recall, our driver didn't seem the least bit concerned for their safety.

At the conclusion of her lively interview of us two young Americans, she *had* initially thought we were RSA military, she needed to turn off the main road. The lady let us off, but not before making sure we had her contact information, along with an invitation to come for dinner when we returned to Johannesburg. That was a promising start to our journey.

An old man in a pickup next gave us a ride for a short distance. He was also friendly and interested in our story, American teachers from the Congo on vacation, but only took us a short ways. After a brief wait by the road, a middle-aged couple then picked us up. When they finally let us off they also offered to host us for a meal upon our return to Jo'burg.

We were very impressed with the friendliness of our drivers and the positive way they described their country to us. We concluded that the white South Africans we had met were *great* representatives of the benefits of living in that beautiful and expansive country. I doubt we could have found black South Africans with the same level of enthusiasm at that time.

Jim and I had covered barely a hundred miles or so of the distance to our destination by mid afternoon. As we stood by the road waiting for a ride, I wondered out loud "What's going to happen if we *don't* make it to Durban by nightfall?"

About the time we were reflecting on this troubling prospect, our next ride pulled up. A slender, young British-South African man pulled up in a small, square

Morris Mini car. As we piled in he asked us our destination. When we replied, "Durban" he smiled and offered, "I'm going that direction as well. I'm headed home for the holidays from my job in the city."

We introduced ourselves, talked about our experiences teaching and living in the Congo, and asked him about life in South Africa. He was a warm and cordial fellow. What followed was an interesting and engaging conversation. Before we knew it several hours had passed. It was nearing sunset when we approached our driver's turn off outside of Durban.

Hitchhiking to Durban with new South African friend

Our new friend then made an interesting decision. "You know, I've always wanted to go surfing on Christmas Day. I think I'll just go ahead and drive you guys all the way into Durban, stay the night and hit the waves before heading off to my parent's place in the morning."

Jim and I were both delighted and relieved that our new friend had decided to escort us all the way to our destination. It was a relief that we wouldn't be spending Christmas Eve standing beside a dark highway somewhere in rural Africa. Serving as a roadside snack for a lion or jackal is not my idea of welcome adventure. The three of us stopped for a meal at a roadside café before heading on towards our resort city destination.

It was fully dark by the time we finally crossed the city limits of Durban. We drove through the main part of town and after a short cruise past the famous beaches, pulled into the entry of a promising motel. It was fully booked. So were the next several we stopped at. This was getting more than a little worrisome.

Finally, we stopped at a motel and asked, implored, the manager if he had *any kind of space* we could occupy for the night.

"Even a closet will do."

"This is high season here in Durban," the man at the reception desk pointed out, shaking his head at our lack of foresight.

"I have nothing available and unfortunately no suggestions for you fellows either. Sorry."

This was *not* good. Dejected, the three of us sat in the Morris Mini in the parking lot and tried to think of what to do next. It was Christmas Eve and *there was no room at the inn.* At *any* inn. It seemed pretty ironic, somehow.

It was Jim who finally remembered that we had a phone number in our possession for someone who lived in Durban. It had totally slipped our minds up to that point. *"Elsie Peters* is her name. Let's give it a try. What do we have to lose?" We found a phone and I dialed up the number. It was well after 11 pm by then, closer to midnight.

A woman answered the phone after a few rings. There was noise and music in the background. I quickly introduced myself and explained our predicament: we were visitors, knew no one in the city and needed help finding a place to stay for the night. Elsie apologized for the background noise. She was having a Christmas Eve party for some young people who were part of a Bible study group she led.

"No problem" was her comment on our need for a place to stay. "We'll just set you three young men up at the missionary guesthouse across town."

She then asked our current location and indicated that someone would come by shortly to lead us to the guesthouse. She would plan to meet us there.

When I hung up the phone and explained to Jim and our young South African friend what arrangements were in the offing, both were greatly relieved and surprised. Especially our driver. He could not get over the fact that complete strangers could be so quickly and graciously accommodated.

"With just a phone call? Late at night, no less! Unbelievable."

We commented that this was not unheard of in the Christian community. He repeated several times that he just couldn't believe it. He had never heard of such a thing.

Subsequent events unfolded just as arranged. After a few minutes a young couple drove up. We introduced ourselves, and then piled back into the little car. They escorted us to a big two-story house in a residential area of town. A lady was waiting for us on the porch as we drove up and she greeted us warmly as we emerged from our vehicle.

Elsie Peters was a friendly middle-aged Canadian woman with an easy and open manner. She introduced us to the guesthouse hosts and assured us that we could stay for several days at the residence if we wished. We should just plan to make a modest donation to cover laundry and breakfasts. She then left assuring us: "I'll be in touch."

Our South African chauffer also spent the night there. He got up early in the morning leaving us a note of thanks. Just as he had planned, the note indicated he was headed for the ocean to get in some surfing before driving home to be with his family on Christmas day. He thanked us for making it a special Christmas for him. The feeling was more than mutual.

When Jim and I woke that morning we both agreed that this was surely the most unusual Christmas day of our lives and that we had already received a very unique set of Christmas gifts.

41

Adventures in South Africa

=•«◎»•=

"Distance not only gives nostalgia, but perspective and maybe objectivity."
– Robert Morgan

On November 21st 1967, General William Westmorland, head of U. S. forces in Viet Nam, made the following comment to newsmen regarding the progress of the War: *"I am absolutely certain that whereas in 1965 the enemy was winning, today he is losing."* By the end of January, 1968, the Tet Offensive shocked the American public as the largest military operation by either side struck over 100 cities and towns in a bloody initiative thought impossible based on the rhetoric of our politicians and military. We 20-something American youth were becoming disillusioned with our leaders who seemed to distort and misrepresent truth in a manner especially costly to our generation.

On December 3, South African surgeon Professor

Christiaan Barnard performed the first successful heart transplant at Groote Schuur Hospital in Cape Town. The world celebrated this achievement and the local news media in South Africa repeatedly lauded this astounding achievement of their native son. December 11th recorded another international milestone, the unveiling of the Concord supersonic airliner in Toulouse, France. Technology was on the move and at an ever-accelerating rate! Only eighteen months later man would actually *walk on the moon* (Apollo 11).

In that season of my life it felt like the pace of significant change was dramatically increasing. What would happen next?

By the end of 1967, Mohammed Ali had had his Heavyweight Boxing Championship title lifted and his draft-dodging conviction was on appeal, a consequence of declaring himself a conscientious objector to the Viet Nam War. In the U. S., post-Christmas hype was building for Super Bowl II, Packers vs. Raiders. On December 30th the Beatles single *"Hello, Goodbye"* hit the top of the charts in the U. S. This compensated for the concurrent but disastrous film debut of their *"Magical Mystery Tour."* These were some of the cultural and popular markers that colored our post-Christmas context in 1967.

As we vacationed in South Africa during that holiday season and interacted with a variety of people from other countries, the Viet Nam War, music and athletics topped the list of conversation topics initiated by those we met, especially the young people. We therefore had repeated reminders and incentives to pay attention to what was happening in the world.

It was clear to both Jim and me that our perspectives on life had been broadened significantly over those which we had imported from home not even two years earlier. We were repeatedly asked to explain how Americans viewed the War, race relations, U. S. foreign policy, and even music and art. We had never been asked such questions before. In fact, we had never even *considered* them, so initially we didn't know how to respond.

As the questions continued and we had repeated occasions to think through and process our responses, we grew in our capacity to identify and explain our points of view. It was actually a very positive if unplanned form of personal development. Cross-cultural encounters may not be a guaranteed antidote to ethnocentrism but they clearly provide the opportunity for developing an appreciation of diversity.

That was our experience, anyhow, in 1967 South Africa.

We stayed in Durban for five days. The mission guesthouse that housed us was an affordable and more-than-satisfactory solution to our need for accommodations. Elsie Peters was an impressive hostess and role model. The group of young people she had befriended stopped by each day to pick us up from the guesthouse and show us the city and its famous beaches. They were a fascinating assortment of young people, all in their early to mid-20s.

One fellow had been a mercenary before he converted to Christianity; another was the runaway son of a German millionaire; a young couple had lived very amoral lives prior to their conversion but had reconciled with God and each other. They virtually radiated joy. The youthful circle of friends were a mix of ethnicities: French, Austrian, British and South African, all gathered by word-of-mouth invitation to join a Bible study led by the middle-aged single lady from Canada.

Mission guesthouse, our residence in Durban

Elsie had opened up her home and heart to these young people and in her low-key, authentic, non-threatening manner had interested them in knowing the reason for her hope and enthusiasm for life. Her engagement with them had been a transformational experience. Elsie's meeting of our need for a place to stay on Christmas Eve was just a taste of the warmth and generosity that this circle of friends had experienced in full measure. We were very impressed.

We were also about to receive even more from our South African hostess.

42
Unexpected Generosity

"A generous heart, kind speech and a life of service and compassion are the things which renew humanity."

– Hindu Prince Gautama Siddharta

A fter several days of exploring Durban, visiting outdoor markets, daily sun bathing, swimming in the warm Indian Ocean surf and getting our hormone-inspired eyes full of South African bikinis, we were ready to consider a change of venue.

As if on cue, Elsie approached us and asked if we might be interested in accompanying her on a little road trip to Zululand through Swaziland. She wanted to visit some friends in a small mission station, drop off some supplies and then drive on to Johannesburg. She indicated that our company would be most welcome since undertaking such a voyage over rural roads was less safe for her as a woman travelling alone. We were delighted to have a chance to see some new country and besides, that drive solved our problem of how to get back to Jo'burg.

We piled our bodies and bags into Elsie's small white pick-up the next morning and headed out for Zululand. It was a bumpy, dusty ride that took us over narrow roads and from open grasslands into curvy, hilly terrain. We had a good time visiting with Elsie about her experiences living and traveling in South Africa as we bounced and flopped around the cab. Was it better to keep the windows open, circulating air, or closed, to shut out the dust?

The first evening, as sunset neared we came upon a group of seven or eight rhinos grazing only fifteen feet away from the road. Wow, we really *were* in Africa!

Jim & John accompany Elsie to Zululand

As we approached our destination that evening, we picked up some native workers and gave them a ride to their village. We then stopped for something to eat at a small restaurant before turning into the mission station nearby where we had arranged to stay the night. As we got up to head for bed, Jim and I discovered that both of our coats were missing. This might not have been too serious a loss except that our money, passports, health cards and plane tickets were all in our coat pockets. We were sure that the jackets must have been taken from Elsie's open truck when we went in to eat.

We prayed about the situation, feeling sick and pretty desperate. "Help!" We had no clue what we might have to do to get back to the Congo from rural Zululand with no money, no plane tickets and no identity papers.

First thing the next morning Jim and I hurried back down to the restaurant to check on our missing jackets. What a surprise. We discovered that the workers had inadvertently picked up our coats with a pile of other things they took out of the truck and our jackets with all their contents were returned intact.

Relief doesn't seem an adequate enough descriptor of our reaction to this most welcome development. We concluded that that had to be as concrete an answer to our prayers as we were likely to *ever* experience. I think I'd still have to agree with that appraisal over forty years later.

Our road trip with Elsie took us back to Johannesburg. She delivered us to the residence of an elderly white-haired widow friend of hers, Celia Moerdyk who lived in a sprawling ranch-style home in the suburbs of the city. It seemed mansion-like in size and quality. She had arranged for the three of us to stay there: Elsie, for just one night before heading back on the main highway to Durban, and we, for as long as we wished.

When we first met this devout Christian woman we got an interesting introduction to white culture in South Africa. As we were visiting over tea in Mrs. Moerdyk's living room, the phone rang. Our hostess answered and expressed regret to the caller that she was unable to keep her appointment that afternoon because she was entertaining guests. When she hung up we naturally inquired as to what we were keeping her from.

"Target practice," was her reply. "Twice a week we ladies go to a shooting gallery and practice our aim. We want to be prepared when the revolution begins."

Celia Moerdyk then pulled out a drawer and proudly showed us her collection of pistols.

Jim and I were stunned. Even elderly ladies, Christians at that, practiced with pistols so that they could defend themselves *when*, not *if*, "the revolution" began? The disconnect with our pacifist perspective, our Christian values and indeed our alternate service commitment left us speechless.

This gracious lady housed us for the next three nights, feeding us big meals and introducing us to a number of her Christian friends. The grounds surrounding her large home were carefully groomed and the garden had little stone pathways with Bible verses posted here and there. Shady benches were located at various spots for rest and contemplation. It was a beautiful, serenely peaceful environment though in truth, Jim and I were hoping for a bit more excitement than relaxation. We didn't have long to wait.

One couple Mrs. Moerdyk introduced us to, Max and Anna Müller, seemed particularly impressed with us and entertained by our tales of teaching in Congo and adventuring in South Africa, shared over afternoon tea. They later called back to inquire as to whether Jim and I might be interested in accompanying them on a short trip to Kruger National Park to see some wild animals. The Müllers had a retired physician friend who lived just outside of the park in a big house, swimming pool equipped, and we could all stay with him and take day trips into Kruger to see the animals. Max and Anna generously offered to cover any costs.

Of course, we were *delighted* with this new opportunity. Indeed, it proved to be a wonderful success of an excursion. We were able to view elephants, giraffes, lions, antelope, Cape buffalo and many more kinds of African wildlife up close. We had a grand stay at the Müller's friend's home and were treated like royalty. This was certainly above and beyond anything we had ever hoped to be able to see or do on this trip.

Max and Anna drove us back to Johannesburg via Pretoria, the capital of South Africa. Beautiful city. Kind and generous people.

While our gracious hostess, Mrs. Moerdyk had been insistent that we return to her place when we got back to Jo'burg, we thanked her as sincerely as we could and let her know that there were some things we had hoped to do in the city in the last couple of days before our plane left for the Congo. We had several dinner invitations pending from our hitchhiking experience and we hoped to be able to go to some English-language movies before returning to Francophone Congo. Mrs. Moerdyk was a very conservative Christian, however, so we left out the movie part when making our excuses. We didn't think she'd approve.

We returned to the same "Hotel Frugal" we had found at the beginning of our trip for our last two nights' stay in South Africa and once again indulged our appetites on food items that weren't available in the Congo. As planned, we also attended several first-run movies. These included *The Comedian, A Man for All Seasons*, and *Privilege*.

What I can recall about our selection of films is that thankfully they were *not* at the same end of the quality spectrum as our initial selection, *Valley of the Dolls*. All three of the films we viewed at the end of our stay were intense, thought-and-emotion-stimulating dramas. Jim and I had some good exchanges as we reviewed our reactions to the story lines. The movies prompted thought provoking impressions on relationships, moral choices and the influence of government to carry back with us and share with our fellow teachers in Kinshasa.

We had one further surprise awaiting us at the end

of this epic vacation journey. Our three-hour flight from Johannesburg landed in Kinshasa in the early afternoon of January 4, 1968. Reluctantly braving the familiar humid, pungent aroma of Congo once again, Jim and I stepped off the plane and headed across the tarmac toward the main terminal. As we walked along, we saw that there were scores of people lined up on the observation deck. The cheering, waving crowd included colorful groups of similarly clad Congolese men and women, some sporting MPR handkerchiefs around their necks and others attired with garments displaying President Mobutu's image. There were welcome banners – *"Bienvenue"* – hanging, uniformed police everywhere and at least the side of the terminal facing the tarmac had received a fresh new coat of paint.

A patriotic welcome back to Kinshasa

"Wow, what a welcome," we mused to each other as we headed into the building. "To think, we've only been gone a couple of weeks!"

Once we cleared customs and immigration our first question posed to our TASOK colleagues who had come to meet us was, "What's going on here?" The answer became clear momentarily. A few minutes later music and cheering began in earnest, as U. S. Air Force #2 landed and Vice President Hubert H. Humphrey arrived for an official state visit. It was his fourth stop on a 13 day, nine-nation African tour. It ended up being a controversial visit, HHH encountered student protesters, but the timing of the Vice President's arrival offered Jim and me a uniquely warm welcome back from our holiday adventure.

I've thought at length as to how I might best summarize the impact of our South African Christmas vacation on Jim and me. Intellectually, emotionally, spiritually we were stretched and challenged far beyond our comfort zones. We realized that something significant had changed in the way we saw others and ourselves. Just what that entailed and how it would affect us in the future still needed to be integrated.

I do recall clearly that I found it difficult to step back onto the plane for our return flight to Kinshasa. Like other "mountain top" experiences in life, I wished I could somehow just stop time and savor it all. Put off reality. Shades of Peter's reaction on the Mount of Transfiguration: "Lord, it is good for us to be here. Shall

I build some shelters to stay a little longer?" (Matt. 17:4, my paraphrase)

I offered the following comments to Betty Jean in my first letter written on our return to the Congo from South Africa:

"It was hard to get back but I really do feel refreshed spiritually and physically. All the things that happened fit together so well and we saw so much more than we could have possibly expected to for such a small expense (aside from the plane ticket, total spent = $50!!). Perhaps you'll understand therefore why Jim and I both feel that the Lord was really with us; why we feel humbled if not awed and so very thankful."(1/17/68)

43

Endings Are New Beginnings

"A time comes when you need to stop waiting for the man you want to become and start being the man you want to be."
– Bruce Springsteen

Have you ever found yourself fully engaged in the present but living emotionally in the future? It's a kind of schizophrenic existence that one realizes at the time cannot be sustained, but given the right set of circumstances, irresistibly settles in like the fog on a bog. That would aptly describe my state of mind during the last six months of my two-year assignment in the Congo. I was plenty busy with activities and responsibilities both at TASOK and in the Kinshasa expatriate community, but I was already looking ahead, working on a new dream.

My thinking about a future career path during the fall of my second year in Africa moved me in the direction of considering a return to the University of Oregon to complete a teaching credential. My summer experiences in Pai Kongila had permanently erased any thoughts of pursuing a medical career. A measure of success in my TASOK classroom had transformed my negative thinking about teaching as a career choice. Maybe it wasn't such a bad idea after all.

By January when we returned from our South African Christmas adventure, I had yet another option to consider. It seemed that my friend and fellow TASOK teacher, Dave Klaassen, had written a strong letter of recommendation on my behalf to his alma mater, Tabor College, after learning they were in search of an admissions counselor. He felt I would be *a natural* for this public relations and recruitment position. With his unsolicited prompt, the Director of Admissions at Tabor inquired into my interest.

Affiliation with a college, extensive travel, contacts with youth, all of these job factors I found very appealing at that age and stage of life. Working and living in a new part of the country, the Midwest, also seemed like a new kind of adventure. In retrospect, I suspect a part of my interest may also have been the realization that Kansas was a lot closer to Wheaton, Illinois, where Betty Jean was in school than was Oregon.

By March I had made a decision. I signed a contract with Tabor College. My dream was evolving.

As I reflect back on this decision now, I see it as completely congruent with Levinson's descriptions of the developmental stage he titles, *"Entering the adult world."*

His research found that young men between the ages of 22 and 28 attempt to establish a life structure that is flexible yet stable enough to allow them to get on with the business of making something of themselves. That's exactly how I viewed the admissions counselor position. It wasn't an end goal but a good next step. I was taking action on establishing myself as a full-fledged adult.

. . . .

If my summer experiences in the interior of Congo were not enough to turn me away from a medical career, I did have additional help. The final test of my medical aptitude came in a specific incident.

One Saturday I accompanied the TASOK junior class on an outing to the campus of the University of Lovanium, in the hills overlooking the city. This former Jesuit university, presently known as the University of Kinshasa, had a beautiful venue with big trees, shaded lawns, a sparkling clear swimming pool, well-stocked snack bar and tennis courts. The TASOK high school students had received permission to use the facilities for an afternoon of recreation and picnicking. As the junior class sponsor, I was *the adult* in charge of supervising a raucous and enthusiastic group of thirty-some teenagers.

It was a blisteringly hot day in the Congo, typical for the time of year, but the heat and humidity did little to modify the antics of the hyper, energized 16-year-olds. There were lots of squeals, cannonball splashes, chases and throwing one another into the pool. At one point, however, the excitement level dropped sharply. A small group of anxious girls brought one of their classmates over to where I sat in the shade sipping a coke.

Junior class outing to nearby lake -- action packed

The young girl in the center was bent over in pain, crying and holding one hand by the wrist with the other. As the troubled cluster of girls neared my deck-chair, their concern became evident: the little finger on their injured friend's hand was sticking out at a 45-degree angle. They all spoke at once, explaining what had happened. The injured girl just whimpered and moaned softly.

"Not to worry," I confidently assured the sobbing girl and her classmates, "I had first-aid training in college, plus I was an assistant to the Athletic Department trainer at my university. It's just a dislocated finger that will readily pop back into place."

Having established my credentials, with an air of confidence that effectively masked my private alarm at the injury, I positioned the girl's arm under mine. I pulled firmly and evenly on her misplaced finger. She let out a howl that is probably still echoing at some back corner of the globe. Startled but undeterred, I repeated my efforts to reposition the errant finger a second time.

At this action the girl's howl turned into a *scream* that brought my first-aid efforts to an abrupt end. Not being completely absent of common sense, I determined the time had arrived to locate the university's infirmary.

The Congolese doctor at the Lovanium infirmary examined the sobbing girl's hand and started to grasp her finger as I had done. The girl half yelled and cried, "No, no...it hurts so bad. Don't pull it!" The doctor paused thoughtfully, then turned and directed his nurse to take an X-ray. The results?

You guessed it. The finger was *broken*. My best judgment was flawed. If anything, my efforts at being helpful had only made things worse for the hapless victim. My lack of innate medical instinct had been confirmed.

If this disaster wasn't enough evidence from one day's experience to flee from a medical career, John Pearson, provided the clincher. A redheaded, fair-skinned son of Baptist missionaries from my hometown of Eugene, John didn't know when to come in out of the sun. By the time I took notice of him and voiced a warning he was virtually *glowing* bright tomato-red. Our day at the Lovanium ended with John being hospitalized due to excessive sunburn.

What ever made me think I should be a doctor? My revised career plans were validated.

44

Preparing to Depart

*"Each man should frame life so that at some future hour,
fact and his dreaming meet."*

– Victor Hugo

Part of forming a new dream for the future involved planning the trip home to the states. These thoughts and fantasies occupied my mind most frequently during quiet times in those last months.

Through discussions with other young adults Jim and I learned that if citizens lived outside of the U. S. for more than eighteen months they were eligible to purchase vehicles in Europe and to import them tax and duty-free. Hmmm. We'd be 24 months away from the States by the date of our return. That got the wheels rolling in more ways than one!

If we could choose any kind of vehicle to purchase under these circumstances, what would it be? The answer was quick in coming, *a sports car*. We were thus

prompted and motivated to spend several weeks re-
searching cars, costs and logistics. The outcome of our
fact-finding efforts was carefully scripted requests Jim
and I each made of our parents to loan us the funds to
buy new cars.

At the time, and even now, it seemed like a real
stretch to approach our parents for a car loan. Neither
of our families were particularly well off financially
and with our futures ill-defined, we had to privately
admit to one another that we were pretty early in our
journey of life to be seriously thinking about acquiring
new vehicles.

Our fantasy was to purchase new sports cars, use
them to tour in Europe, then ship them to the U. S. and
drive them across the country to our homes. It was a
23-year-old's pipe dream and we ventured to put it out
there, fully expecting to receive kind but firm denials
from our financially conservative, practical-minded
Depression Era parents.

Much to our surprise and delight, our hopeful but
unlikely petitions were successful! *Both* of our parents
agreed to make the funds available for car purchases
at the end of our stint in Africa. They must have loved
us a lot to over-ride their almost certain objections and
participate in this indulgence.

Working through a well-known auto broker, Transol
Car Sales in The Hague, Netherlands, Jim proceeded to
order a white '68 Triumph Spitfire Mk III for around
$2,600 and I ordered a hunter-green '68 MGB with wire

wheels for $3,200. That seemed like a lot of money at the time. This was a *really* big deal. Brand new sports cars? Travel in Europe? Start our next chapter with *panache*? How could we stand to wait!

While the prospect of acquiring new sports cars was arguably the most exciting element in our plans, making travel arrangements to tour Europe came in a close second.

Our travel plans took the following form: Our exit from the Congo would be via Alitalia Airlines departing from Kinshasa on June 8 right after school was out. We would first head to Rome, then on to Florence and Amsterdam with short stays both places. We would take possession of our cars in the Netherlands and travel for 21 days in a loop through Europe, staying in youth hostels or whatever cheap lodgings we might find along the way.

Spurning the formation of a specific itinerary, we planned to "wing it" and get ideas for travel destinations from people along the way. By July 7 we would return to Amsterdam to ship our vehicles to New York. We planned to fly to London on July 10th for a couple days of sight seeing and then depart for the U. S. on the 12th of July. Our cars would arrive in New York by the 16th or the 17th. At that point, we would begin our trek across the country, speculating that we would finally make it home to Oregon a week or so later.

Plan set.

45

Social and Spiritual Wrap Up

*"Maturity doesn't come with age;
it comes with acceptance of responsibility."*
– Ed Cole, Christian Men's Network

Visions of cars and travel danced in our heads. There were still, however, plenty of responsibilities and activities competing for our attention in the final few months of our sojourn in Africa.

In addition to regular classroom duties at TASOK, it seemed like a myriad of scheduled events filled each weekend and some of the weeknights as well. Junior class and church youth group outings occupied some weekends. My duties as a sponsor of both groups dictated participation in their activities. On any free weekends we attended first-run American movies at the U.S.I.S. facility.

In February the annual Valentine's Day banquet was held at the Union Mission Hostel. It was a dress-up affair and over 100 persons attended. Jim and I were there in body but not especially in spirit. Our dates for the evening, a fellow teacher and the school secretary, were friends but definitely not love interests.

We also made an appearance at TASOK's all-school talent show, held in March. I played a borrowed ukulele, Jim played his guitar and we sang Simon and Garfunkel hits. Our apologies to Simon & Garfunkel. The two of us also served as auctioneers for the spring fund raiser.

Auctioneer team Jim & John in action

Jim led the drama production of "Arsenic & Old Lace" and co-directed the spring musical, "Oklahoma." In the latter case, there was added drama in the week leading up to opening night, as both of his leads became ill, costumes had not been completed and there were serious technical problems with the lighting. Somehow, it all came together in the end. The critics, parents, raved.

The final school events of the year included a faculty/student soccer match that nearly killed off those of us teachers foolish enough to participate. It didn't take long before I wished I had given the student star, Dave Schaad, a better grade in biology. The concurrent fish-fry fundraiser was equally dangerous, the undercooked fish was barely edible and those of us brave enough to partake, wished we hadn't a little later that same evening.

The TASOK school year ended with a junior/senior banquet at a fancy restaurant in the outskirts of Kinshasa. Graduation exercises followed a few days later, concluding a whirlwind of year-end activity.

In our final months in Congo, as previously noted, our thoughts had clearly shifted to the future. One may safely conclude from this listing of activities, however, that Jim and I were far from bored or detached from our circumstances. While we had relatively few *commercial* diversions, no TV, no cell phones, no iPods, no fast food, and few movies, we were engaged in a wide variety of meaningful events that were very people oriented.

I don't believe I can recall another period of time in my entire life that was ever scheduled any fuller than those last weeks in Africa, but that was at the same time, any more valuable or fulfilling in social/emotional terms. I would be remiss in my description, however, if I didn't address the evolution that had taken place in my spiritual interests and perspectives, manifest in those final weeks.

I sometimes wonder if God doesn't answer our prayers and strengthen our faith in more concrete ways when we are young than later in life. I seemed to experience many answers to prayer in those days. Perhaps it could be said that our Western affluence and American efficiency places us currently in a less God-dependent position with regards to everyday needs and challenges than was the case when living in Africa. Then again, maybe it was merely the idealism of youth that pointed my attention to circumstances I interpreted as "signs," or "specific answers to prayer."

However one might choose to analyze it, my last months in Congo were animated by a keen sense of God's presence and guidance. I was very enthusiastic about my faith and willing to share this perspective with whoever might listen. That included Congolese.

Jim and I determined that our spiritual experiences in Africa were missing an important element, direct contact with nationals. We attended an English-speaking church each Sunday since neither of us spoke either French or Lingala, the two official languages of the Democratic Republic of the Congo. Our language limitations kept us in a virtual cultural cocoon. In an attempt to break this self-imposed isolation, I had begun to acquire a minimal Lingala vocabulary, mostly on my own initiative, practicing with the Congolese workers at TASOK. I was far from fluent in the language, however.

At one point, to rectify the above deficit in our experience and to satisfy our curiosity, Jim and I arranged to accompany veteran missionary, Rev. Arnold Prieb, to Sunday services held in a chapel on a local Congolese army base.

The first Sunday, at Rev. Prieb's prompting, Jim brought his guitar and phonetically employing a Lingala hymnal, sang and strummed a couple of familiar hymns before the audience. I borrowed a trombone from Prieb's family and accompanied Jim with brass harmony. Guitar-trombone music may seem like a pretty weird combination, but it *worked*. Much to our surprise and relief, we received an enthusiastic response from the 75 or so uniformed Congolese soldiers and their colorfully attired wives who were in attendance.

"That went pretty well," we said to one another.

Rev. Prieb overheard our response. With a twinkle in his eye he upped the ante: "That was OK for *this* Sunday's effort. However, we've been invited to return again next week. Next Sunday the pastor wants to hear not just your music, *but also your testimonies.*"

Jim quickly opted out: "I'll stick to the music, thank you very much."

"I can't speak Lingala well enough to give a testimony," I meekly protested.

I suppose I must have been pleased enough with myself for learning a few words of Lingala that the testimony request flattered me, bypassing both my resistance and good sense. Prieb cheerfully offered to review my words if I would just write them out and be willing to present them in the next week's chapel service. He thought that it would be far more effective for me to communicate my story in Lingala than for him to translate my words from English.

"Well, I suppose I could try," somehow slipped out of my mouth.

As soon as I said it, I wished I hadn't.

All the next week I sweated out what I might say. How much does a 23-year-old American pacifist Christian have to say to a Congolese army crowd, anyhow? I somehow ended up scripting a couple of short paragraphs, which Rev. Prieb quickly reviewed and OK'd on the drive to the army base the next Sunday. In retrospect, I'm not sure how helpful his appraisal was since he actually didn't know Lingala very well at all. He was fluent in a different Congolese trade dialect, Kituba.

When it finally came my turn to stand before the chapel crowd, I was genuinely sweating and not just because the service was indoors. As I began my speech, the enthusiastic Congolese pastor who shared the dais, rose and began to embellish my words. Whenever I paused to take a breath, the sparkling-eyed African cleric jumped in, repeating and expanding on my points in a loud and animated manner. After each phrase I uttered, he injected his detailed explanations, clarifications and animations. I think that's what they were, at least. He easily outdistanced my Lingala vocabulary.

Whatever they were, judging from the crowd's reaction, they were *way* more interesting and entertaining than *my* words. He solicited "Oo's" and "Ah's" and loud "Uh's" from the fully engaged audience. He was on a roll. His dramatic flair hit a crescendo when he emphasized it was my *faithful obedience to God's direction* that brought me all the way to Congo to teach children. Rev. Prieb offered that interpretation to me later. Actually, that particular point wasn't part of my written message.

When I finally came to the end of my scripted words and took my seat, I received an enthusiastic Congolese ovation. I recall being as confused by what had just happened, as I was relieved that it was over.

You'd think that I learned my lesson about public speaking at the Congolese Army base. Not so. Youth Sunday was scheduled at the Kalina Protestant Church and that put the youth group in charge of the service. The sponsor of the youth group was expected to offer the morning message.

That would be, *me!*

I have no lingering recall of what the theme was for

that particular Sunday morning or just how the youth might have been involved in the service. One only remembers selective details so many years later. I chose to present my talk from a music stand on the stage rather than to climb up to the formal elevated pulpit on the side. It was my best shot at humility.

I remember rising to present the morning message, looking out into the faces of the nearly 500 congregants and wondering how many pairs of eyes belonged to seminary trained pastors and missionaries who would be critically appraising my words. "Why did I ever agree to do this?" cycled and recycled in my brain.

I took a deep breath and began. Somehow, repeated theme in my life, *it all came together in the end.* I survived, people said nice things to me and I made it out alive. My enduring sentiments were *gratitude,* for not screwing up, and *relief,* for just getting through the experience, rather than any kind of pride at how well I seemed to be serving God.

. . . .

The final weeks and then days of my two-year Congo experience at last drew to a close. A strange kind of nostalgia set in. It dawned on me that I had come to genuinely appreciate the place. Africa no longer seemed like a foreign land; it had become my home. I realized how much I had learned: about teaching, about culture, about responsibility. These were freshly evolved perspectives. I had come to understand my identity in ways that had new meaning for me. I did not feel like the same person any longer. My goals had shifted. I had acquired new skills. I could communicate in another language, minimally, to be sure, but passably. I could travel and survive in unfamiliar places. I was able to cook, wash, clean and care for my daily needs. I could teach and lead young people. My relationship with God was more personal. I was more self-confident.

I had become an adult.

These thoughts made the final farewells even more poignant. Jim and I were booked for meals in the homes of friends and colleagues virtually every night of our final two weeks in Kinshasa. Our excitement about the future was tempered by a genuine sense of loss. We had come to experience a compelling sense of community in our two years there. The time had arrived, however, to turn the pages on this chapter of our lives and head for home.

But where was home? Neither Jim nor I planned to settle in Oregon. We were each going to have to make use of our newly acquired survival skills and create new homes for ourselves. It was in this mixed frame of mind, pleased but unsettled, that we headed for Europe and the last weeks of our great adventure.

Year two Christian Service unit: Amy Dahl,
Garry Schmidt, Ruth Klaassen, John Franz, Lois Schmidt,
Jim Becker, Elaine Bonnet and Dave Klaassen

46

A Roman Reprise

"When you leave Africa, as the plane lifts, you feel that more than leaving a continent you're leaving a state of mind. Whatever awaits you at the other end of your journey will be of a different order of existence"
– Francesca Marciano, "Rules of the Wild"

T he Congo dawn rose on cue at 6 am on our final morning in Africa, illuminating the sky in bright orange, red and yellow hues as if to celebrate the special meaning of the day. This wouldn't be my final Congo color serenade, I'd return to Africa in five years for a second two-year stay, but at the time, the morning sunrise had a kind of nostalgic finality to it.

Piled in the middle of my apartment's tile floor were my bags, packed and ready to load up for the drive to the airport. All of the personal effects that had made this space home, my home, from the time the walls went up, were gone.

Some of my personal baggage, however, was not in the pile on my floor. For the second time in as many years, I was about to encounter a destabilizing experience that would alter my self-perception. This time, however, the identity being vacated, at least in part, was one in which I had a greater sense of ownership. I had largely inherited my sense of self during my formative years. In contrast, this identity had been shaped by insights and choices I made in response to the many novel challenges and people I encountered in Africa. It was part and parcel of my first adult life structure.

Now, with symbols of my Congo-based identity packed away or shipped off, I was about to return to my home culture. A new self-consciousness about that culture and my relationship to it dawned on me at that point in time. I would not be returning home to occupy the role I had left. That role no longer existed.

Living in Africa had changed me and I would certainly approach people and circumstances differently going forward. But I also understood that I was leaving the world of TASOK teaching that had become both familiar and rewarding. All that I had acquired these past two years would not accompany me on this journey, either. I would need to once again construct new relationships with friends, colleagues and institutions.

That thought was a bit unsettling, mildly anxiety provoking. But paradoxically, it was also exciting and hopeful. Who knew what the next chapters of my life would offer, education, career, marriage? Much was still ahead in life to be discovered.

With these thoughts and emotions swirling in my brain, Jim and I joined the line of missionaries and TASOK teachers boarding the Alitalia Air flight from Kinshasa to Rome in early June 1968. Since we knew so many of our fellow travelers and since virtually all were heading home or on vacation, spirits were high on the aircraft. Few remained in their assigned seats for the entire flight.

The seven-hour flight was over before we knew it. Having departed at noon, it was still daylight when we landed, not nighttime as our internal clocks expected. Roman sunsets in early June take place at nearly 9 pm, almost three hours after Congo's nightfall. This change signaled to us that we had indeed left the world of the tropics. On this, our second visit to Rome, we had a pensione reserved ahead of time and a plan for how we wished to spend our days.

Things had changed in two years: not Rome, *us*!

In the two days we were there, we retraced our prior visits to many of the prime tourist spots in the Eternal City. The highlight of our Roman holiday, however, had to be our tour of the Vatican. After viewing Michelangelo's magnificent pieta statue in the huge interior of the Basilica of St. Peter, we climbed the stairs to the roof, amazed at the size of the façade statuary: Christ, St. John and the eleven apostles all towered over 18 feet high. They had looked so tiny from the ground far below. Everything in the entire structure seemed bigger than life.

We were also flabbergasted at the commercialism and the blatant marketing of religious icons in the Vatican. For a price, we were informed, we could have our gift shop purchases blessed by Pope Paul VI himself, a service he apparently performed on a daily basis. These and other claims by our tour guides stretched our appreciation of religious authenticity in the Holy City. Based on this particular exposure to the faith, we young Mennonites speculated that we'd have to work hard at suspending our disbelief to ever become good Catholics.

Another highlight of our time in Rome involved joining the crowds in St. Peter's Basilica Square to receive the Pope's blessing. Skeptical? Yes, but we'd never have a chance to test the impact of a papal blessing if we never received one. The crowd swelled as the hour neared for the pope's appearance. Jim and I serendipitously met up with Joel and Lucy Janzen, fellow TASOK teachers who had traveled with us to Rome. We spied them at some distance across the square and made our way through the masses to join them for the blessing.

The Janzens were there with their two children, five-year-old Greg and seven-year-old Julie. Greg was placed atop my shoulders to get a better view of things as we stood among the thousands gathered there. We all stared up at the right window of the top floor of the Apostolic Palace, waiting for Pope Paul VI's appearance.

John & Greg (on shoulders) wait for Pope's appearance

Unclear what this was all about, Greg innocently asked, "What's going to happen?"

I quietly confided in him, "In a couple of minutes someone will drop a red cloth out of the window and then this man will step into the window frame and flex his muscles for all of us to see."

"Cool!" was my tiny companion's delighted reply.

A few minutes later, the red velvet cloth did indeed drop to the cheers of the crowd, and a man, Pope Paul VI, did step into the window with his arms held high as he blessed the crowd in several different languages, spoken in succession. Apparently, however, not all of us received a blessing from the Pope's appearance. Recalling the scene many years later, the Janzens assured me that Greg had been *very* disappointed that "the guy in the window" never actually flexed his muscles as expected. Regrettably, I must bear the full weight of that misinterpretation and any accompanying disillusionment remaining over the years since then.

Our next stop was a brief one in the art mecca of Florence. We flew in and out on the same day. Our whirlwind tour included stops at the famous 13th Century Duomo Santa Maria del Fiore, and the Piazza della Signora with Michelangelo's replica of The David statue. Quick stops at additional art galleries, churches and exhibits soon overloaded my limited capacity to absorb art and history. It was embarrassing to hurry through these fantastic, world famous venues. It seemed disrespectful to merely scan such quality and depth of beauty and history.

Perhaps it was due to our effort to cram too much into too little time, but by late afternoon we missed our flight connection. Just when we were resigned to "have to" stay overnight in Florence – there *are* worse places to stay – KLM came through and rebooked us on a later flight to Amsterdam, our next stop.

47

The Auto Tour Begins

"A journey is like marriage.
The certain way to be wrong is to think you control it."
— John Steinbeck

Our Europe tour began in earnest with the acquisition of wheels. What also commenced was a pattern of travel that would define our entire experience. We began with a general sense of what we wanted to do and where we wanted to go, but as we actually started to implement our plans we were often forced to innovate and flex. Obstacles arose, circumstances changed and opportunities unfolded in unexpected and unusual ways. To us at the time, this was an adventure of the highest order.

Mr. Hertzog, the broker from whom we had each purchased our new vehicles, was there to meet us at the Amsterdam Airport Schiphol together with his wife. Our original plan had been to drive my new MGB in Europe for three weeks, but Hertzog regretfully informed us that a production delay at the U. K. factory had rescheduled the delivery date of my vehicle. He did, however, have Jim's white Triumph Spitfire gassed and ready to go so that our travel plans did not need to be altered.

We had no problem with this change, though I was disappointed in the unexpected delay meeting up with my new car. Mr. Hertzog was very unimpressed with British efficiency and minced no words conveying his disgust at the missed delivery of my vehicle.

We had arranged in advance for hotel lodging in Amsterdam but after we completed the details of our business arrangements, the Hertzogs asked if they could take us out to dinner. We followed them in Jim's racy new sports car to a fancy restaurant not far from the airport.

What followed was a first class meal, featuring raw fish (Jim and I somehow managed to get it down) and a very engaging and enjoyable interchange with our gracious Dutch hosts. They insisted we top off the meal with "jenever", aka Dutch gin, and got a big laugh from our grimaces imbibing the strong liqueur as novice drinkers.

In the end, the Hertzogs made us promise we would stay with them on our return to Amsterdam at the end of our European circuit.

We were in great spirits as we retired to our hotel that evening. A new sports car, gracious hosts, Europe to explore: it was enough to make one's head spin. Or maybe that was just the gin.

From Amsterdam we began our drive south to Brussels, Belgium. It was a warm morning when we set out and we had the top down on Jim's Spitfire. Several times in the three-hour drive, when the traffic slowed people honked, waved at us and yelled things in Dutch.

"What was *that* all about?" I wondered out loud. We finally figured it out.

Since Jim's Triumph had been purchased in The Netherlands and had a "NL" sticker on the back, Dutch people assumed us to be fellow countrymen. We had this experience repeatedly throughout our tour of Europe: smiles, waves and "Hup, hup, hup!" Dutch folks sure seemed to be exuberant, enthusiastic people!

We actually had an objective in our Brussels visit: to contact Dan and Anne Erickson and their son, Ted. The Ericksons were well-known veteran missionaries with the Evangelical Covenant Church, having served in a variety of educational and administrative capacities in the Congo. Their son, Ted, had been a student leader at TASOK and a former member of my basketball team his junior year. The Ericksons had taken on a special assignment in Brussels for Ted's senior year.

Our error in pursuing this reunion mission was forgetting to bring along the Erickson's address. We spent several hours and made numerous stops in our efforts to locate them. With our minimal French applied to the max, in the end, we were successful. It proved to be a good first test of our ingenuity on the road. Jim and I arrived just in time to attend Ted's graduation exercises from the American School of Brussels. We spent the night celebrating his commencement and enjoying the Erickson family's hospitality. The next morning we headed for France.

As we climbed into the Spitfire that morning, the Ericksons warned us that we might want to avoid big cities in France, especially Paris. The news in recent days had been filled with reports of widespread strikes and violent clashes between students, unions and the police. The Hertzogs had given us a similar warning.

Having been completely out of touch with world news, this latest warning was sobering. Vacationing in France could mean we were heading for trouble.

The unrest in France had actually begun with a series of university student protests in May 1968, and it culminated in parliamentary elections that consolidated the Gaullist government's power by the end of June. This resolution came in response to the largest general strike ever, involving two-thirds of the nation's workforce, one that virtually crippled the French economy and threatened to bring down President Charles de Gaulle's government. Leaders feared civil war or revolution.

It was a historic moment when the nation's moral consensus shifted from conservative to a more liberal ideal. This iconic shift in the basic moral principles of French society is referred to today simply as "Mai 68."

By the second week of June, when we arrived on the scene, demonstrations were waning. On June 16 the police retook the Sorbonne in Paris in a final bloody clash that ended the rebellion. After some discussion, the two of us travelers concluded that our sense of adventure clearly did not extend to fighting Paris traffic and dodging violent demonstrations. It was disappointing to miss seeing this famous locale.

We made a big detour around the City of Lights and eventually found our way to the lovely city of Chartres fifty miles south of Paris. This city contains the medieval Cathedral of Our Lady of Chartres, a beautiful High Gothic cathedral adorned with twin spires dating from the 12th and 16th Centuries, respectively. It is a popular tourist destination. Its famous resident relic is the *Sancta Camisa*, said to be the tunic worn by the Virgin Mary at Christ's birth. We contained our skepticism enough to admire the beauty and majesty of the historic religious structure. It was hard to even imagine ourselves in a church that was already over 500 years old when the U. S. was founded.

The following day we drove over seven hours to Toulouse in the southwest corner of France where we found a small two-star hotel for the night. Our drive through rural France was memorable. Each little town had its own steepled church, bakery and outdoor cafes. Most of the farms we passed seemed small and here and there people still used animals to pull carts or to plow. It felt like we had gone back in time. It was wonderful. Fascinating.

Picnicking by France's vineyards

We minimized our lack of French language skill by doing a lot of pointing and applying *"s'il vous plais"* and *"merci"* liberally. This strategy seemed to work well. We prudently consumed continental breakfasts at our lodgings, purchased sandwich makings at small grocery stores for lunches and only dined in restaurants for dinners.

Travel in France was turning out to be a delightful adventure, not a hassle as some had warned.

Three and a half hours drive from Toulouse the

next morning brought us to Spain's Costa Brava and the small seaside resort town of Tossa de Mar, our destination. I don't remember who originally told us about this place but based on the recommendation we had been given, we expected "inexpensive and scenic." We weren't disappointed.

For under $10 a night, our simple lodging included breakfast and dinner. One savory evening's entrée was a rich, cheesy lobster casserole, my first ever. The sandy beaches were lined with bikini and speedo-clad Europeans, and the quaint village boasted Roman ruins and a fortified medieval "old town" dating from the 14th century.

On our own, touring the Spanish Rivera, this was living!

Two activities we novice travelers associated with Spanish culture, a bullfight and flamenco dancing, highlighted our two-day stay in Tossa. The bullfight we witnessed followed a traditional Spanish pattern. Three matadors each killed two bulls in the course of the afternoon. Their skill or lack thereof at dispatching the huge animals earned them the cheers or jeers of the audience.

Trumpets and a band introduced a procession of the afternoon's bullfighters accompanied by their colorful retinue. As soon as they cleared the arena, a bull came charging in. Each bull was worn down first by the respective matador's fancy cape maneuvers and then by lance stabs from picadors on horseback. Finally, agile performers on foot stuck banderillas, colorful barbed stakes, into the bulls' shoulders. Each featured matador then re-entered the ring with a small red cape and a sword to finish the kill. The first two matadors in our day at the bullfight were miserably unable to kill their bulls after repeated stabbings and bloodletting. The crowd booed as the picadors finished off the pitiful creatures. A tractor dragged the dead carcasses out of the arena. The final matador proved to be the most skilled, by dispatching each of his bulls with one deft thrust of his sword, to the wild cheers of the crowd. An ear from the slain animals was cut off and presented to the victorious bullfighter as his reward. The matador bowed deeply and waved. The crowd cheered loudly. The band played. We just sat silent, stunned and thoroughly disgusted.

Attending a bullfight proved to be a very disturbing experience overall and not one that either Jim or I ever had any interest in repeating. I later read that in 1989, Tossa de Mar was the first town in the world to declare itself an *anti-bullfighting city*, an action that came about twenty years too late for our queasy stomachs that summer afternoon.

Perhaps queasy stomachs marked the theme of our Spanish entertainment, since it also accompanied our evening of viewing flamenco dancing. The performance itself was very impressive. The elaborately dressed dancers spun, clapped, clicked and stomped to the lively, rhythmic guitar music. We sat so close to the central wooden stage that we could feel the vibrations from the dancers dramatic stomps and see sweat rivulets running down the faces of the male performers. The nausea part came from drinking cheap champagne that accompanied the nightclub's cover charge. Neither of us had acquired much of a taste for alcohol and so by the end of the evening our appreciation for this entertaining cultural experience was tempered by the effect of the cheap booze.

Our initial experiences with independent travel in unfamiliar circumstances were very fulfilling, even energizing to us, with the possible exception of the bullfight. If this could be considered a test of how far we had come in our ability to adapt and enjoy the challenges of the new and novel, we were passing with flying colors! In contrast to our initial travel experiences just two summers earlier, our anxiety was minimal and our motivation to explore and discover was elevated.

We repeatedly shared this observation with one another as we made our way along. It frankly felt good to pair an increased sense of self-confidence with ever-more-frequent speculations about what might be ahead of us on our return to the States.

Beach & Roman ruins at Tossa de Mar

48
Europe Part Two

"One's destination is never a place,
but a new way of seeing things."
– Henry Miller

F rom Spain we headed north to Switzerland. The first part of our drive took us up the scenic coast through the French Riviera cities of Perpignan and Montpellier before we turned inland toward the Alps, passing through Valence. At the end of a long eight-hour day of driving we finally arrived in Geneva, windblown and bleary-eyed. We stopped at one of the many "zimmer frei" (bed and breakfast) signs we passed along the road. Fortunately for us, the hosts spoke some English so that's where we spent the night. Switzerland was expensive. We determined we would not linger.

Our three days in Switzerland began with a drive along Lake Geneva, viewing the famous Jet d'Eau (water spout) and on to the lakeside Castle of Chillon, which we toured. Venturing further into the Swiss Alps, we arrived in Interlaken. Nearby we took a dramatic cable ride to the top of the Shilthorn, a 9,700-foot peak with panoramic views of many famous alpine peaks including Jungfrau, Eiger and Mount Blanc. The rotating restaurant at the summit is the location where the classic James Bond thriller *"On Her Majesty's Secret Service"* was filmed a year after our visit. The cable car ride alone was worth this diversion.

It's a long way down from the Shilthorn

Zurich marked the endpoint of our Swiss tour. It was there that we decided no visit to this country would be complete without acquiring a "world famous" Swiss watch. We made our purchases.

I have to smile in retrospect at how often on this trip we made decisions with minimal information, operating mostly from stereotypes and travel tips we acquired along the way. We were pretty unsophisticated travelers. Neither Jim nor I had had much previous exposure to other cultures; we were sorely lacking in any international context or in having any bases of comparison. The watch purchase illustrated this point, a decision based more on a stereotype than from any researched facts.

Our tour of Germany began with a visit to Bavaria, Munich to be more specific. No visit to this city would be complete without a stop at the Hofbräuhaus, a huge beer hall with long wooden tables and benches. Arguably Munich's number one tourist attraction in the city center, we included it in our agenda of sites to see. The beer in this place was only served in huge one-liter containers, giant pretzels helped to soak up the suds and an ompah brass band played traditional Bavarian tunes.

The atmosphere was loud, raucous and merry. People we met were very friendly. The more beer served, the friendlier they got. One group of German drinkers at our table invited us to stay with them at their ski chalet. Unlike our boisterous red-faced German tablemates, the beer wasn't our main interest, the people were. It was easy to get caught up in the fun atmosphere.

We visited two impressive castles during our time in Bavaria. One was Neuschwanstein Castle, also known as the "castle of the fairy-tale king." Once the residence of the shy king Ludwig II, it was crowded with tourists who, like us, wanted a first-hand look at this storybook dwelling in an idyllic setting. We were told that over six thousand visitors toured the castle each day in the summer. That seemed an accurate estimate the day we were there.

We also visited the huge 17th century Nymphenburg Palace during our stay in Munich. Everything was lavish in this amazing place from the elaborately groomed park of nearly 500 acres, to the gilded carriages in the museum on the grounds. As impressive as the palace was, I have to confess that I was more intrigued by viewing the huge Glockenspeil (clock tower) in the Munich town hall with its 43 bells and 32 life-sized moving figures. That was entertaining as well as unique.

From Munich we decided to visit Berlin. In 1968, Berlin was an isolated city behind the Iron Curtain. It was a six-hour drive even taking the super fast autobahn. Driving in the slow lane at 80 mph, we were the slowest vehicle on the road. The string of Mercedes and BMWs that screamed by us were all traveling at well over 100 mph. Autobahn driving was impressive and a little scary. At those speeds wouldn't *any* accident be fatal?

High fences lined the entire autobahn route since it sliced an insulated corridor through East Germany. On the other side of the fence we observed farmers cutting grass with hand scythes and oxen pulling carts piled with straw. These images posed a dramatic contrast to the modern, highly mechanized farms we had just driven past in West Germany.

During our brief stay in Berlin we searched out directions to one of Germany's most famous landmarks, the Brandenburg Gate, along with the nearby Reichstag or historic parliament building. We also made a point to visit the Berlin Wall to check out "Checkpoint Charlie," the best-known crossing between East and West Berlin during the Cold War.

John chats with East German escapee at The Wall

Jim and I stood by the ominous concrete wall, quietly observing that it stretched as far as we could see in each direction. We could clearly view armed East German soldiers moving slowly back and forth on the other side of the gap. We wondered what it must be like to live under oppression and to be so desperate for freedom that one would risk getting shot in order to escape. While we were pondering this thought, a German man standing nearby turned to us and struck up a conversation in very broken English. He proceeded to tell us his story about escaping from the East, but with his strong accent and limited English vocabulary we had a great deal of difficulty following his comments. What did come through, however, was his deeply felt passion for freedom and his gratitude for having safely escaped to the West.

"Man, this place is an eye-opener for me. I can't believe how much I take for granted!" I commented in later conversation. Jim agreed.

"That includes our freedom to travel to this very location," he observed. "Where does Mennonite non-resistance fit into this picture?"

It was good food for thought.

From Berlin we originally intended to visit both Denmark and Sweden, perhaps even Norway, but our time was running out. We determined we could make but one more stop before heading back to Amsterdam to get our cars on a boat to the U. S. A ferry took us from Germany to Denmark and a short drive brought us into the capital, Copenhagen. It was a beautiful city, clean, colorful and full of activity. We visited Tivoli

Gardens, Europe's second most visited theme park behind Disneyland, and toured the city, including a pilgrimage to the seaside statue of the "Little Mermaid," a national icon derived from poet and novelist, Hans Christian Anderson's tale of the same name. In the evening, we visited a club and listened to American jazz singer Eartha Kitt perform. With only one full day in Scandinavia, we figured we had done as well as we could in our choices of what to take in.

It took us a full day of hard driving to return to Amsterdam. Mr. Hertzog was waiting at his office with good news, my forest green MGB had arrived and was in the warehouse. I needed to just "take possession in Europe," i.e. to drive it around the block so that I could legitimately fill out the U. S. customs/import papers. What a thrill to finally slide behind the wheel of that new sports car.

After a fouled sparkplug was cleaned, my new car purred smoothly and Jim and I drove our vehicles to the nearby shipyard for transport to the U. S. Once this was accomplished, we had two more days remaining before heading off for London and on to the States.

Mr. Hertzog had previously invited us to stay with him for this "down time" and he was true to his word. What he had in mind was a bit of a surprise to us, however. He asked if we'd like to join his grown son and daughter on an excursion to the family houseboat that they had parked on a canal some distance from the city. Hertzog and his wife would join us in a day or so.

We gladly agreed and soon we found ourselves in their powerboat speeding along a network of canals, through flat lands and by windmills until we finally arrived at their houseboat, parked in a wide spot along a canal. For the next two days we occupied ourselves waterskiing, sunbathing, eating and visiting with the Hertzog children, both in their early 20s. It was a wonderful, relaxing respite from the hard driving pace of our European auto tour.

Our down time on the Hertzog's houseboat provided a good opportunity for Jim and me to reflect on what we had just experienced. Some of our reflections had to do with recounting the amazing venues we had visited and the spectacular, scenic images we had seen. Others had to do with identifying the challenges we had met: food, lodging, communication, directions and problem solving. We had been surprisingly successful in our efforts.

Perhaps our most poignant reflections, however, were closer to home, more personal and psychological. We struggled to find ways to describe to each other how our observations and encounters had altered our perceptions. Our biases, assumptions and reactions had surely been impacted in our travels. Prior expectations of others and ourselves no longer fit so snugly. A successful and rewarding auto tour through Europe was a confidence booster, to be sure, but it was also humbling and amazing to consider how well things had worked out, planned or not. Our stay with the Hertzogs was just the latest example. This experience left us feeling blessed and carried by God. What an unexpectedly satisfying conclusion to two years of Christian service, we mused.

On that positive note, after a two-day respite with the Hertzogs, we boarded our flight for the short hop to London. Perhaps now our travel challenges were all behind us.

Perhaps not.

Windmills lined the canals in the Netherlands

49

Mennoniting Our Way

"There is an emanation from the heart in genuine hospitality which cannot be described, but is immediately felt and puts the stranger at once at his ease."
– Washington Irving

Our preparations for departure from Amsterdam to London did nothing for Mr. Hertzog's negative opinion of British institutions. It seemed that British Air, our carrier from The Netherlands to the U. K., had more restrictive baggage allowances than our previous airlines. Thus, we had to repack our luggage, discard some clothes, wear multiple layers and carry on heavier items in order to consolidate our checked luggage into two bags each. Hertzog was thoroughly disgusted. Jim and I simply did what we had to: we adapted, where we had no alternative and proceeded on our short flight to London without further delay.

Before we left the Congo, we had arranged through

Menno Travel to stay at the London Mennonite Centre, a large private dwelling located in the northeast side of the city. It primarily served as student housing for young people attending university in London from third world countries. The Centre was founded in the mid-1950s, as a positive response to housing discrimination experienced by students from the former British Empire, principally India and Africa.

Quintus and Miriam Leatherman, an American couple originally from Philadelphia, were the Centre's gracious hosts at the time of our visit. We occupied the clean and simply furnished guest rooms during our visit. It was a convenient place to stay in London not only because of affordability but also since it was close to one of the main rail lines and to bus service.

One of the Centre's traditions was afternoon tea, a fascinating opportunity to interact with the diverse mix of nationalities residing there and to talk religion and politics. The expanding Viet Nam War attracted lively questions and comments directed to us young American pacifists. No boring exchanges here!

What does one see with only two days in London? Our agenda choices may not have been creative, but at least we were consistent, our selections were trite, predictable but satisfactory to us. We toured the historic Tower of London, site of Her Majesty's Royal Palace and Fortress. We checked out the crown jewels and royal mint that are housed there. Of course, we witnessed the changing of the guard at Buckingham Palace and visited the magnificent St. Paul's Cathedral, the first major edifice built after the British Reformation. Finally, our list included viewing Westminster Abby, the traditional site of the British royalty's coronations, weddings and burials.

By this time, I felt overdosed on magnificent religious structures. I had acquired what one tour guide cynically identified as the "ABC" state of mind: *"Oh, no! Not Another Bloody Cathedral!"* We had seen so many grand churches in our travels that they were all starting to morph into one another in my memory. It was time to leave Europe. We were anxious to arrive on American soil once again.

London's Big Ben says it's time to head home

Jim and I exchanged smiles as our KLM jet touched down at JFK airport in New York. We weren't prepared to break into song, like our Italian travel companions had done two summers before, but we *were* glad to be back in the U. S. once again. Customs was a breeze compared to our Congo experiences. Clearing the official station, my quietly spoken Lingala phrase, "Malamu, pensa!" Very good!, brought a knowing smile of agreement from Jim. Soon we were on an airport transit bus headed to our drop off point at the Grand Central Station in midtown Manhattan.

We had not made any arrangements for our stay in New York City. The arrival date for the ship transporting our cars from Europe was two days away. Though we had acquired a good deal of travel confidence and experience along the way, in retrospect it still seems a bit naïve or shortsighted not to have lined up lodging in advance. I felt I had matured greatly, but it is obvious that at age 24, I still lived in the moment much of the time. Our lack of forethought on where to stay illustrated that.

We stood at the busy station pondering what to do next.

"Why don't we look in a phonebook and see if we can find anything 'Mennonite,'" I finally proposed. "Maybe *someone* will give us a safe recommendation of where to stay."

I had imagined that perhaps New York City had a Mennonite church and pastor we could solicit for advice. I had begun to recognize the value of networking. This was a big city and we were not big city people. Regrettably, that particular insight had dawned on us a bit late.

We didn't find a church in the phone book, but we did come across a listing for "Mennonite Voluntary Service Center" on East 19th Street in Manhattan. We called the listed number, explaining to the young voice that answered the phone, that we were two Mennonite fellows completing our alternate service, in need of a place to stay for a couple of days. The young woman on the other end of the line was very gracious: "You're in luck. We have a couple of guest rooms available for just this sort of thing. You fellows are welcome to stay with us. Just hop on a bus and head straight south from where you are to our place on E. 19th Street."

That sounded easy enough. However, since we hadn't yet changed our travelers' checks into U. S. currency, we didn't have bus fare. We decided to walk from Grand Central Station on 42nd Street to the four-story Menno House on E. 19th. It didn't seem *that* far by the numbers. This was not a wise choice.

By the time we had hauled our heavy bags the 25+ blocks to our destination on that hot, humid July afternoon, we were absolutely thrashed, dripping with sweat. Exhausted. An upbeat trio of VS workers was there to greet us and show us to one of their upstairs guest rooms. They told us we were fortunate no one tried to stop us on the way, two walkers with all that baggage made easy targets. We were fortunate. And naïve.

We spent the next three nights at the Menno House. The small group of a dozen "VSers," as they called themselves, was scattered at various work assignments during the day: youth centers, hospitals and nursing homes, mostly. In the evening their communal dinners were lively, punctuated with humor and story telling. One of the young men told of being robbed on the way home from his service site that first day. Two others informed us they had had similar experiences in recent days. We were sobered. Service was not only risky in African settings.

Our hosts were interested in our Congo experiences as well. These peer exchanges were rewarding opportunities for Jim and me to begin interpreting our experiences of the past two years, to reflect on their significance, on what we had learned and how things had changed for us. Those sharing opportunities were the best part of our stay.

The worst part of our sojourn at Menno House was the weather: it was unbearably hot and humid the entire time we were there. There was no air conditioning in the residence and we just *sweltered*. We lay on our narrow twin beds each night with the windows wide open and we sweat. During the days, we decided our best strategy to find some relief from the oppressive heat might be to head for the waterfront. We took ferry rides to Staten Island one day and to Liberty and Ellis

Islands the second. The breezes over the water helped.

On our first evening back in the U.S. I phoned my parents. They were delighted to hear my voice once again and eager to know about our schedule for the long cross-country drive home. I informed them that we didn't know for sure when our cars would arrive and that we hoped to make some short stops along the way to visit people we had met in the Congo. Thus our exact arrival date home was unclear, it would be at least a week or ten days from then. "Get home as soon as you can," was their terse reply.

As I hung up, I realized that I felt a twinge of resistance in having to once again face my parents' expectations after two years of detachment from them. It was a familiar paradox of young adulthood: I looked forward to seeing them, but I wasn't eager to have my independence tested.

Jim and I had anticipated a two-day stay in New York before the freighter's scheduled arrival with our cars. It ended up taking another full day before we received a call back telling us they were ready to be picked up. It was an eagerly anticipated reunion. I'm sure the excitement of the moment was evident, had there been any on-lookers: with a flourish we put down the ragtops, fired up our engines and motored west on our homeward trek.

50
Heading Home

*"There is nothing like returning to a place that remains
unchanged to find the ways in which you yourself have altered."*
– Nelson Mandela, "Long Walk to Freedom"

The last few days marking my return home might be anticlimactic to describe except that they not only culminated a significant period of growth and development in my young adult life, but they also marked the beginning point of decisions leading to life-long commitments I was to make in the areas of career and intimacy, work and love.

From New York City Jim and I headed southwest to Akron, Pennsylvania. Mel and Anita Penner, former staff from Menno Travel Service in Kinshasa, had relocated to that city and we thought a short overnight stay with familiar folks would make a good first stop on our homeward journey. We had gotten a late start from the shipyards and it was only a three-hour drive to this location. After a good meal and visit with the Penners, and with Garry and Lois Schmidt who had also stopped in on their way home, we borrowed sleeping bags and bedded down on their lawn, our choice, that night. At first light the next morning we planned to hit the road.

Before settling down for the night, I worked up the courage to call Betty Jean in Illinois where she was attending summer school at Wheaton College. I had received encouraging letters from her before I left the Congo, but I wondered if she would still be interested in seeing me when the time to visit actually arrived.

Happily, I received my hoped for response: an enthusiastic invitation to stop in for a visit. "I've already asked my folks and you are very welcome to stay at Mom and Dad's place here in Wheaton," she offered.

BJ's parents had only recently returned to the U. S. from the Congo and had relocated to Wheaton to be close to her and her sister, Beverly, who was teaching in a nearby suburb. She gave me directions to their house. I told her to plan on my arrival the following evening.

That next day was a killer in terms of miles covered and time behind the wheel. From Pennsylvania we headed up through Ohio and Indiana, only leaving the freeway every couple of hours to use roadside restroom facilities, to gas up or both. By late afternoon we had caravanned as far as Toledo, Ohio, on Interstate 80/90. This was our parting point, as Jim headed south and I continued further west toward the Chicago area.

The sports car caravan across the U.S. begins

Jim's journey took him to Indianapolis for the night and then on to Kansas. He had arranged to spend a few days with his brother and family who were living in Wichita. After my visit with BJ, I was expected to meet my new employer at Tabor College, just north of Wichita. I also needed to go there to line up a place to live when I returned to Hillsboro in August to begin my new job. Jim and I planned to join up once again in a few days and continue on our drive to the West Coast and home.

Seeing BJ once again after a year's absence was all I could have hoped for and more. In spite of being wind burned, bleary-eyed and in a near hypnotic state after twelve long hours behind the wheel, I was thrilled to find Betty Jean rushing up to my car as I pulled up to the curb. She gave me a long hug and in a completely unselfconscious move, kissed me. I kissed back!

Betty Jean was a vision. A sight for my (literally)

sore eyes! If anything, after a year in college, she had become more attractive than I remembered her; that's what I thought at the time. Her parents greeted me warmly and welcomed me into their home and into their lives, as it turned out. Neither BJ nor I ever seriously dated anyone else after this rendezvous.

What transpired in the next several days was a blur of conversations, tours of the college and community, meals together, reminiscing and catching up on our respective experiences. We rediscovered the value of our communication, that we could share even difficult or troubling topics openly and comfortably with one another. And we could laugh at ourselves and with one another, as well. Betty Jean was someone with whom I could resonate, someone whose values and life experience were compatible with my newly formed, Congo-framed identity.

I learned that BJ had experienced a kind of reverse culture shock in her return to the States for college. Growing up overseas, she had missed out on many cues from mainstream American culture; it was not easy to fit in. Academics were tough as well. She was attending classes with high achievers in a very competitive environment. BJ had had a tough first year of college. On the plus side, she had new work and service experiences, spiritual growth opportunities, supportive roommates and a beautiful college venue.

I appreciated Betty Jean's genuine interest in me as well, as I described my second year of teaching, our recent European travels and shared my mixed emotions about starting a new job in a tiny town in Kansas. She was a good listener. Our romantic moments in the warm summer evenings were pretty special, too. Though the Fourth of July was well behind us, there were still fireworks! I may not have officially crossed the "falling in love" line during this visit, but I had clearly become infatuated.

The unexpected attraction and thrill of my reunion with Betty Jean simply made time stand still for me. All of a sudden, I discovered I had been in Wheaton four full days! I needed to re-connect with reality. I had several calls to make: to Tabor College where I was expected to make a showing; to my parents who were wondering where I was; and to Jim to arrange for our planned travel rendezvous.

Sweet reunion in Wheaton on the drive back

The first call was the easiest to make. Dr. Wiebe, my new boss, was pleased to hear from me. He let me know that a "meet and greet" potluck had been arranged in two days hence so that his staff and others in the Tabor College community could welcome me and two other new hires. That meant I had one more day to spend with BJ. I'd then need to leave very early the following morning to complete the eleven-hour drive to mid Kansas and still arrive in Hillsboro by the scheduled dinner hour.

My next call was to my parents. I knew this was not going to be easy and I was right. Both of them immediately came on the line. Mom blurted out her burning question: "Where *are* you, John? Outside of town? Somewhere close?" She didn't wait for me to reply before continuing, "Your sister and brother-in-law have been here with us for a week, waiting for your arrival. They only have a few days of vacation left before they have to head back home. They're anxious to see you; *we're* anxious to see you. We've been worried. What has happened?"

I realized that my explanation was not likely to appease my family, but it was overdue and needed to be made. I took a deep breath and launched into it. "I'm still in the Chicago area, Wheaton, to be specific. I stopped here to see this African girl I met in the Congo. I haven't told you about her, but I'm pretty interested and wanted to spend time with her, so I stayed a couple of days longer than I had originally planned. I'm sorry you were worried."

"What?" was my father's reply. "*An African girl?*"

My mother, gracious person that she was, immediately chimed in, "Well, John, any girl you fall for must be a *fine* person," her voice trailed off in a question mark.

"You did what?" my dad injected, in an incredulous tone.

I imagined Dad was about to reference the warning speech he had previously delivered prior to my leaving home. I did *not* want to go there. Besides, I was enjoying this ruse.

"Perhaps I should clarify," I continued, "She is a blonde-haired, blue-eyed missionary kid, born in Congo. Her parents are Mennonites from Mountain Lake, your birthplace, Dad."

I went on to explain how I knew the Rempels and their daughter, Betty Jean, and that she was currently attending the well-known Christian college. Had I not been concentrating so keenly on what I was saying I surely would have heard both of my parents' audible sighs of relief.

After a few more questions and answers, I moved on to inform them about my scheduled social function at Tabor College in two days. Our conversation ended with Mom repeating her plea: "Don't take unnecessary risks, but please *do* make every effort to get here as soon as you can." I agreed I would do my best.

My last call of the evening was to Jim, updating him on my reunion with BJ. He was very amused with my report, especially the story of how I had managed to startle my parents by announcing serious interest in "an

African girl." I also informed him about the Tabor pot-
luck and that we'd need to hightail it back to the West
Coast ASAP since I had simply taken too much time
hanging out in Wheaton. He thanked me for the information and agreed we'd have some long days of driving
ahead of us if we were to push the pace getting home.

Did we push the pace? Beginning the morning after
my potluck with the Tabor folks, we drove 22 hours
straight from Hillsboro, Kansas, to Winnemucca,
Nevada. Other than the usual pit stops for food, fuel
and relief we made only one unscheduled stop on the
drive home.

Our unplanned stop came in the middle of a pitch-
black night in rural Colorado and was prompted by a
black and white cow that stood in the middle of the
road as I rounded a sharp bend. I slammed on my
brakes and my new MGB did a complete 180-degree
spin out. By the time Jim rounded the bend behind
me I was off the road in a cloud of dust and the cow
was nowhere to be seen. My guardian angel must have
earned his wings on that one! We tried sleeping following that incident but the adrenalin from the near miss
kept us from doing so. On we drove.

At Winnemucca we finally reached our limit. We
had made good time in Nevada with no posted speed
limits, but I could simply no longer focus my eyes or
my mind. It was dangerous. We were dangerous. We
checked into a motel and collapsed, utterly exhausted,
for eight hours of dreamless sleep.

The next morning, over coffee and eggs at the Denny's next door, we said our goodbyes. Each of us had an eight-hour drive ahead to complete our cross-country trek, but it was hard to finally part and go our separate ways. It was no longer a Congo dawn we shared, but a Nevada sunrise. A new day was indeed dawning in our lives. It was a bittersweet realization. We had come such a long way together. We were not the same pair of fellows who boarded the train together two years earlier. I suspect on some level we realized that from here on in life we would be on our own, or form new alliances.

A manly hug later, Jim climbed into his Spitfire and headed off in the direction of his brother's place in California and I made a beeline for Oregon.

I clearly remember slowly driving the last mile to my parent's home in Eugene. Strangely, I no longer considered it to be *my* home. That was a novel thought in itself. It was late afternoon, the end of July and the shadows of the long row of maple trees on Grove Street reached across forming a kind of orderly lattice as I slowly cruised along, deep in thought, convertible top down in the warm summer air.

The trees on that familiar lane had grown a good deal in my two years' absence, as had some of the bushes and landscaping along the route. Much of the drive was familiar, nearly the same in appearance as I had remembered, *or was it?* Did the same people live in the houses I was passing? Had some of their children left to start their own lives as I had? Were they smarter, wiser, richer, or healthier than when I last passed by?

What had transpired in the lives of the inhabitants? One couldn't tell just from looking, how much change had occurred in two years. It dawned on me that the same thing could certainly be said of me as well.

With that thought in mind, in two more turns I was in my parent's driveway once more. The sign across the front porch railing read *"Welcome Home Kinshasa Kid."* I leaped out of my car to embrace my impatiently waiting family: Mom and Dad, my very pregnant sister and my brother-in-law.

This journey had come to an end, but curiously it had the feel of a new beginning.

Kinshasa Kid is welcomed home

Epilogue

"One can live magnificently in this world if one knows how to work and how to love."

– Tolstoy

E ach day, the Congo dawn brought new and unexpected challenges and opportunities. It seemed we were constantly facing novel circumstances for which we were unprepared. Africa was a remarkable crucible for personal development. But since each day is inextricably linked to the next, I discovered my perspectives had been subtly shaped and matured in unanticipated ways. The cumulative effect was a transformative experience that has endured through my lifetime.

My service as a teacher at TASOK and later, briefly, as an admissions counselor with Tabor College proved to be the portal that led to a thirty-five year career in higher education. At Tabor I became friends with the director of the college's new social work major. Through his influence my interest was piqued and I enrolled at the University of Kansas to earn my Masters of Social Work (MSW) degree. Subsequently, I was recruited to develop an undergraduate social work major at Fresno Pacific College.

During those years I also earned a doctorate at USC. I then went on to work at California State University, Fresno, as the campus' first Director of Employee Assistance and later as a tenured professor in the Department of Social Work Education. Thus, the work experiences and opportunities described in this memoir indeed served both as the introduction and foundation of my life's career trajectory.

A similar thing happened in my love life. Betty Jean and I pursued our interests in one another, begun in Congo and renewed on my drive home. In the summer of 1970 we were married. BJ completed her BA degree at Wheaton College in record time, three years and three summers, to facilitate the timing of our nuptials.

After three years of marriage we returned to Kinshasa for a two-year term with the Africa Inter Mennonite Mission serving as house parents for 20 or so missionary children attending TASOK. It was one of our aspirations from the beginning to return as a couple to the place where we met and to share an overseas living/service position together. In the years 1973 – 1975 we fulfilled that ambition.

The experiences I have described in this memoir also served as a stimulus for a lifelong interest in travel and exposure to other cultures. In the forty plus years of our marriage, BJ and I have returned to Africa three times and traveled in Europe more than a dozen times. My two years of alternate service thus yielded not only a lovely and compatible life partner, but one with whom I could share my newly formed and enduring values and interests. Congo was the portal through which I found love and adventure.

It's not a stretch to imagine that those years of living in the Congo may have also impacted our immediate family in various ways. Our two daughters, Mindy and Kristin, both participated in summer mission service in Africa during their teen years. Mindy went to Liberia in 1987 and Kristin spent the summer of 1990 in Kenya and Europe. Kristin spent time in Belize as part of her undergraduate college major in international studies; Mindy has traveled in a number of countries in Europe, Central and South America.

Noted earlier, Mindy's roommates and best friends in college at FPC were the daughters of two of the Christian Service couples I served with. She currently enjoys a full-time teaching career in higher education. Kristin married the son of a former MB missionary doctor and wife who served in the Congo. She is a writer and Kristin's spouse is a university professor. Ripples of influence have spread widely across our family's pond of life.

Finally, the spiritual experiences and insights formed during my Congo years proved to be good travel companions on my life's journey. They too served as a portal of a kind leading to enduring future commitments to God and to my faith community. Over the years, I have been accompanied by a keen sense of being loved and cared for by my Heavenly Father, a perception I trace back to answers to prayer and outcomes, both desired and undesired, referenced in this memoir. I am humbled and grateful to God as I consider the generosity and creativity of His touch on my life.

It's as if the Congo dawn awakened my soul.

CPSIA information can be obtained at www.ICGtesting.com
Printed in the USA
LVOW090810090712

289189LV00001B/1/P